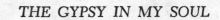

THE GYPSY IN MY SOUL

The Gypsy in My Soul

THE AUTOBIOGRAPHY OF JOSÉ GRECO

by
José Greco

with
HARVEY ARDMAN

Doubleday & Company, Inc., Garden City, New York
1977

ISBN: 0-385-11504-0
Library of Congress Catalog Card Number: 76–23765

THE GYPSY IN MY SOUL

ONE

My earliest memories are of being coddled and cooed over by women—half a dozen buxom, sweet-smelling aunts; a grandmother who doted on me; a warm, protective sister two years older than I; and, of course, Mama, always Mama.

When I was born—two days before Christmas 1918—they made an extraordinary fuss over me. Though my family was large, I was the first baby boy of my generation. So the women took a special delight in me, a feeling I returned entirely.

My early memories of my father and of my uncles are not so vivid. When I was about three years old, Papa left our tiny village and sailed off to America, promising to send for us when he'd established himself and gained his citizenship. Several of my uncles—and many of the other men in the village—did the same.

Over the years, it's been written that I was born in Argentina, or in Spain, either of Spanish parentage or of a mixed Spanish-Italian background. Actually, I was born in Italy, in a little town called Montorio Nei Frentani, in the Abruzzi Molise Mountains, overlooking the Adriatic Sea. And I was christened not José, but Costanzo.

I've never hidden the truth about my birth and ancestry, but I suppose I haven't done enough to deny the myths that have grown up about me. After all, when people go to see a Spanish dancer, they like to think he is Spanish.

But even when I make the facts clear, I'm not always believed. Thirty years ago, when I first danced in Spain, the newspaper critics insisted I must be Spanish, no matter what I said to the contrary. One even called my claim to Italian birth "some kind of publicity stunt." An American then associated with the U. S. Embassy in

Spain, Robert Kieve—now a longtime friend—simply said, "I don't believe it!"

I can't even say that I come from a family of dancers—or musicians. My father was a baker and a son of bakers. My grandmother was known as the oven woman.

There was one musician in our family, however—an uncle we called Lylie. He was also the town barber. I recall sitting at his feet, along with some of my cousins, listening entranced as he played nostalgic songs and beautiful melodies on the guitar, or as he talked of great actors, great singers, and great musicians.

While I listened to Uncle Lylie as he played and sang or simply talked, I gazed at the walls of his shop, which were decorated with pictures and posters of the foremost performers of the day.

On one wall, I remember, were several beautiful photographs of the great Caruso. On another was a huge poster of Rudolph Valentino, the main picture surrounded by little photographs of the actor in his most famous roles.

I was fascinated by all of it. At one moment, I would dream I was Caruso, and another, I would imagine I was Valentino.

The Montorio I grew up in was a beautiful village of about fifteen hundred people. It was set on a series of rolling green hills, under a sky of the deepest blue, within sight of the Adriatic Sea. I had room to run and dozens of cousins to play with.

But Montorio was not so idyllic as it seemed. In my childhood, it was still suffering the aftereffects of World War I. Food—particularly meat and sugar—was rationed.

The modern conveniences were slow in coming to Montorio. Airplanes and passenger liners were all but unknown to us, and we rarely saw automobiles. I must have been four or five years old before electricity came to our town. I can still remember my astonishment at the sight of the first electric light.

With electricity came something else that astonished us—movies. Don Ettore, one of the richest men in town, rented the church basement one night and, for a small fee, showed us films of American Indians. The images so impressed me that they never left my mind.

It was about this time that I had my first encounter with sex. I'd heard the older kids talking about it, and I decided to see what it was like for myself. So I took my little cousin to what I thought was a secluded spot on a stairway and began to experiment. Neither she nor I could have been much older than five or six at the time.

Suddenly, Mama came running up the stairs, yelling at me. Some neighbors across the street had evidently seen what I was up to and told her. Well, my mother gave me a real spanking. I don't think that at that age I could have gone very far, but my mother's spanking only increased my interest.

All I know is that from that moment on, I had a new attitude toward girls. I sensed that every girl I saw might be a potential partner in this still-unknown and undefined kind of pleasure.

Apart from that, I tried to be a good boy, I think. But I got myself into mischief from time to time. Two occasions stand out in my memory.

The first happened one Easter Sunday, when I was four or five. My mother had bought me a new white suit and matching white sandals for the holiday. After the Mass, she told me I could go walking with some of my friends. She knew how proud I felt in my suit and how much I wanted to show off.

My friends and I decided that the best possible thing we could do on this beautiful spring day was to go into the fields and pick ourselves some cherries or apples—and bring some home to our mothers, of course.

We had no trouble finding plenty of ripe fruit. But in walking through the damp field, I got my beautiful new sandals covered with mud. However much Mama was going to be pleased by the fruit, I knew she'd be furious over my filthy, mud-smeared sandals.

So on the way back to town, my friends and I stopped off at the Fountain of St. Constance, a lovely fountain about twelve feet wide and five feet deep. I hopped up on the ledge and dunked my feet in the water.

Then, suddenly, I lost my balance and fell in. Not having the faintest idea how to swim, I was soon in over my head, being sucked toward the outlet pipe that irrigated the fields. I was too big to be drawn through, but too small and too weak to free myself from the suction.

Fortunately, one of my uncles happened to be riding in from the fields at that moment. He must have heard my friends' screams, because he leaped off his horse, threw himself into the fountain, and dragged me out, limp, dripping, but alive.

Another few minutes and there never would have been any Spanish dancer named José Greco. That night, I got a good talking-to from my mother—but no spanking. But I was sad because I'd ruined the beautiful new suit and white sandals.

My other bit of memorable mischief in those days also took place on a Sunday morning. Mama had dressed me up for Communion and left me sitting on the top of a table. She'd gone off to get my shoes.

I soon noticed that a little package of sugar was sitting beside me. Now, sugar was rationed in those days, remember. Besides, I "knew" that it was an unpardonable sin to eat before Communion.

But how old was I—five or six? How could I resist? I opened the package and ate a little lump of sugar (this was before it came granulated) about the size of a pea. Then, realizing the horror of my deed, I broke out into tears.

When Mama returned, she found me sobbing, desperate. I told her I'd committed the unpardonable sin of eating sugar before Communion, that God was going to kill me in punishment.

She pleaded with me to stop crying, but I needed further reassurance. So she took me to the village priest, a good and kindly man who treated all children as his own.

He looked at me and saw the suffering I'd endured and he told me, "Don't worry any more, my child. Come and take Communion. God will forgive you." I felt as though I'd been rescued from hell.

When I grew older, I began school. And to keep me out of further mischief—and to see that I learned a trade—my mother sent me to a local carpenter, a distant cousin, to become his apprentice. Well, his junior apprentice.

Mama didn't realize it, but this man had a terrible temper. What's more, he stuttered. There's nothing wrong with stuttering, of course, but his speech impediment got me into trouble.

Every time he asked me to hand him a tool, I'd bring him the wrong one. I couldn't understand him because he stuttered so much. I was anxious to do right, but I usually did wrong.

The carpenter thought I was making fun of him. So he started to beat me—regularly. And one time he locked me in a wooden box. Before long, I was terrified of him.

One night, he came to our house at about 9:30 P.M. He told my mother that he had to go attend to something in the cemetery and he needed my help. My mother saw nothing wrong with his request. After all, he was a cousin. So I went.

I remember everything about that night. There was no moon at all, and it was very windy. The cemetery was deathly quiet. I would have been frightened in my mother's arms. Accompanied by the carpenter, I was terrified, and more. I felt a terrible, eerie morbidness.

We walked through the graveyard, the carpenter lighting the way with a torch, I following behind with an armload of boards, a hammer, and some nails. Finally, he stopped, stuck the torch in the damp ground, and motioned me forward.

While I watched, scared out of my wits, he fashioned a tiny little casket. Then he took a small bundle out of a shallow grave and unwrapped it. It was a dead infant. He put the infant in the box, nailed it shut, and buried it. Then we both walked out of the cemetery, neither of us speaking.

That night, my mind filled with morbid thoughts, my nightmares began. I don't know what I thought this man was—a murderer, some kind of a ghoul, who knows? But I thought he was unspeakably evil and that he'd somehow involved me in his foul deeds.

Now, of course, I understand what had happened. The carpenter was probably burying a stillborn child, no doubt an illegitimate baby. He was told to keep it as quiet as possible, so, knowing I wouldn't understand, he had me help.

The next day, I woke up with a fever—compounded by an overwhelming sense of dread. I don't know what I imagined, but I felt the carpenter was going to do something to me—hit me, kill me, punish me terribly.

Before I knew it, I was seriously ill. It took me months to recover completely. And even after I started to play outside again, I still feared the carpenter. Whenever I had to pass his shop, I made sure my mother shielded me from view.

Incidentally, whenever I visit Montorio, I see the carpenter. He's still there, a very old man now, looking kindly and a little befuddled —anything but evil.

Throughout these years, I remember my mother getting letters from my father, sometimes accompanied by money, sometimes by little gifts. But there was no request for Mama, my sister Norina, and me to pack our bags and join him in America.

It was June 1928—I was nine—when the big letter came. My father had become a naturalized U.S. citizen, thereby making his children U.S. citizens automatically. More important, he was ready for us to come. He'd even sent a special dress for my sister Norina and a flannel suit for me to wear when we landed in New York.

Our little family packed up and headed for Naples, on the opposite coast of Italy, where we were to depart for the United States. For a nine-year-old boy who'd never been more than a few miles from his home, Naples was quite an experience.

My childhood memory of Naples is that it was a great, enormous city, swarming with joyous people, the air filled with sounds of mandolins and singing. Who could ever forget those songs? I was so impressed by those melancholy strains and sweet laments that even today, I prefer sentimental—even nostalgic—music to any other kind.

The music I heard in Naples has haunted me ever since and has left a permanent imprint on my musical tastes. Even now, when I hear a Neapolitan or Sicilian song, my eyes get a little damp.

But Naples was more than just music. Wherever I looked, there was excitement—a street vendor flinging pizza dough high into the air, carts loaded with all manner of delicious fruits, gigantic silver airplanes flying overhead, miles of streets running off in every direction, thousands of people all jabbering at once.

We stayed that night in a hotel and had dinner there. Since I was underage, they gave me half of everything—half a bowl of soup, half a plate of macaroni, half a portion of chicken.

I tolerated this until it came to the fruit. Everyone at the hotel got one pear and one apple. I got half a pear and half an apple. I made such a fuss about this that my uncle, who was accompanying us, took me to a cafe for dessert. It had a showcase loaded with Italian pastries.

Of course, I can't remember exact words, but as I recall, he said something like this:

"Tomorrow, you're going to America, Costanzo. Who knows when you'll be able to eat Italian pastries again? Help yourself. Have whatever you want."

That night, I ate enough pastry to make up for my entire nine years' worth of sugar rationing and half portions of dessert. I must have had at least fifteen pieces, all huge, all filled with thick, rich, creamy filling.

The next morning, I was deathly ill—or so I felt. My stomach trouble lasted for three or four days, through most of my boat trip to America. As a result, I vowed never to eat sweets again.

In those days, the United States Immigration Bureau had offices in many major European ports. Immigrant passengers bound for America would be checked through these offices, which handled all the formalities. Then they'd board their ships. There'd be no need for further processing once they got to the United States.

Restraining my moans and groans, I accompanied my mother and Norina to the U.S. offices in Naples. There I was thoroughly checked and my head shaved. Then we boarded the ship that would take us to our new home.

Both my mind and my body were in turmoil by now. I had little idea of what kind of life lay ahead for me. All I knew was that I was going to see my father again. It was both exciting and frightening. Then too, I was still suffering from the effects of a stomachful of Italian pastry.

We were given a cabin for four and asked to share it with a rather pleasant, elderly lady. I remember spending most of those first few days on ship in my upper bunk in that cabin.

On the second night out, my nervousness, my fatigue, and my state of restless excitement got the best of me. We were all suddenly awakened in the middle of the night by the old lady who was sharing our cabin—and who occupied the bunk below mine.

"It's raining!" she screamed out, frightened, momentarily disoriented. "It's raining! Close the windows! Put up the umbrellas!"

It wasn't raining. It only seemed that way, because a little boy—off on the biggest adventure of his life—had forgotten his toilet training.

TWO

I don't remember much about that boat trip, but I do remember my first impressions of New York, as we docked at one of that city's West Side piers, then came down the gangplank. It was terrifying.

All around us were skyscrapers that dwarfed even the largest buildings in Naples. The sidewalks were mobbed with people, more people than I'd ever thought existed. And the background noise—the blend of rumbling trucks, angry taxi horns, and roaring elevated trains—made me fear for my life.

And then, up in front of us, I saw a man, a handsome man, looking debonair in his straw hat. He was smiling at us and hurrying in our direction. He was my father. He looked like a god.

As he reached us, he threw his arms around me joyously and kissed me and flung me into the air. Then he did the same with my sister. And finally, he embraced my mother, holding her for the longest time.

My father arranged for our trunks to be put into a taxi. While they were being loaded, he turned toward me and reached into his pocket. He pulled out a fifty-cent piece and four dimes.

"Here, Costanzo," he said. "This is fifty cents and this is forty cents. But this is one coin and this is four coins. Which would you like, the fifty-cent piece or the four dimes?"

Well, I wasn't stupid. I could count. "I like the little ones," I said, choosing the dimes. I'll never forget that.

My father smiled broadly and poured the dimes into my hand. Then he gave the fifty-cent piece to my sister. Then we all climbed into the cab and started off.

We were headed toward Brooklyn, toward Hopkinson Avenue,

where my father was boarding with my mother's brother and his wife.

Even with my entire family beside me, the taxi ride from Manhattan to Brooklyn was a harrowing experience. The traffic, the astonishing hustle and bustle of the city, and the incredible noise was almost more than I could bear.

Back in Montorio, America had seemed like a dream world. Those who'd seen it spoke glowingly of its beauty and riches. Yet what I'd seen was unspeakably ugly. Also, it was incomprehensible. Outside of my family, I hadn't heard a word that made any sense to me. The contrast was shocking.

But once we got over the Brooklyn Bridge—I was too frightened to be much impressed by it—things began to change. The buildings were smaller, the noise level lower. The cars in the streets and the people on the sidewalks seemed to move more slowly.

Soon we were driving among rows of nice-looking houses. I began to relax a bit. But more unpleasant surprises lay ahead.

The taxi turned up a small, hilly street and stopped in front of a house in the middle of the block. There, on the stoop, to my amazement, sat a woman cleaning fava beans.

Now in Montorio, during the fava bean season, many women sit on their stoops cleaning and sorting them. But here, in America, did they also do this? Were there peasant women here, too? It made no sense to me. There were no green hills or fields around.

The woman, I soon discovered, was my aunt, my mother's brother's wife. She was not happy to see us. She rose from her perch and looked at us with restrained dislike.

"You go upstairs," she said. "I'll be there shortly. We'll eat something." No welcome, no "How was the trip?", no "Happy to see you," nothing.

Exhausted, befuddled, I went upstairs with my sister, while Mama and Papa unloaded the taxi. Shortly, the adults came in and we sat down to what turned out to be a terrible meal.

My aunt, it happened, was from Calabria, in southern Italy. Montorio, my home, is in the center. The people of Calabria use very spicy seeds in their food. It isn't exactly hot, but the aromatic odor is too strong for my taste; and as a little boy from Montorio, it was as foreign to me as chow mein.

But I ate. My hunger was too strong. Then, hardly able to keep

9

my head up, I lay down on a leather couch in the living room. The droning of voices soon put me to sleep.

I don't know how long I slept, but I remember my aunt waking me up roughly, screaming and cursing. I'd wet my pants again—and the couch, too, and the floor nearby.

We stayed at the house on Hopkinson Avenue for about six months, during which time I never heard a happy word between either my aunt and my uncle or my aunt and my father. She was impossibly bitter. About what, I shall never know. Perhaps it was the way of southern Italian puritan women.

But it wasn't all bad for me. I had three cousins to play with, and there were other children nearby. And my father often took us to the Canarsie Beach, or to Coney Island.

One August day, Papa had us all dress up in our best clothing—me in the suit he'd sent me in Montorio, Mama in her fur-collared coat (despite the heat), Norina in her Sunday finest. Papa even put on a vest for the occasion.

Then we all went to the photographer's shop on Fulton Street, next to the Paragon Theater. "My family is all together now," my father said, "and I want never to forget it." We spent more than an hour with the photographer, who impressed me as being a nice man.

During the week, however, I saw very little of my father. He spent his days as a laborer on the IND subway, helping to build the part of the line that runs through Brooklyn.

And I also spent some of my summer at work, helping a Montorio *paisano* who owned a shoe repair shop, painting the edges of the new soles and heels black. I think he paid me a nickel a week for my services. I didn't mind. His language brought Montorio back to me, which helped relieve my loneliness.

The neighborhood we lived in was a bad one (though not nearly as bad as it is today, I am afraid). But I was innocent of such things —for a while. One afternoon, my father came home with a gift for me, a scooter. I fell in love with it immediately. I rode it everywhere, even to the shoe shop.

One day, after work, I went to get my scooter, which I'd left outside at the curb. It was gone. I searched for it, thinking I must have put it somewhere else, but it was nowhere to be seen. Then the horrible truth dawned on me: My scooter had been stolen.

I remember sitting down on the curb then and crying. It wasn't simply the loss of the scooter, devastating though that was. It was also the realization of how cruel people could be.

Soon, summer was at an end. It was time for me to start school. My parents took me to P.S. 73, where, since I spoke only a few words of English, I was given a test to determine which grade I should enter. Even though I was nine, the authorities decided I'd better become a second-grader.

We soon moved to a somewhat better neighborhood, still in Brooklyn, taking a house on Herkimer Street, and I transferred to P.S. 155. By that time, I'd caught up with my proper grade—fourth —since I was learning English quickly.

Almost from the beginning, however, I disliked school. I especially disliked my schoolmates, who were always fighting, stealing things from each other, cursing each other, and calling each other names.

And as the newcomer who spoke broken English, I was often the focus of their attention. I couldn't believe it when the other kids— especially the second-generation Italian kids—would call me a guinea or a greaseball.

I couldn't understand why they thought people of some ethnic groups were good and why others were considered bad. I didn't know why they felt they had to belittle some people.

To me, everyone was a human being. Jews, Greeks, Neapolitans, Spaniards, Sicilians, blacks, Puerto Ricans, Frenchmen, Portuguese— none was any better than the other, or any worse. To my school-mates, though, the differences were obvious. This was one of the things that separated me from them.

We moved again, this time to Manhattan, to Fifty-sixth Street, between Eighth and Ninth avenues, then back to Brooklyn again, this time to Cooper Street. Then we moved to Manhattan once more, to a building right next to our former home there. After that, it was back to Brooklyn, to Somers Street, and J.H.S. 178.

In those days, we never stayed in one place for more than a year, at most. Why, I do not know. Perhaps it was a matter of money. I recall that we often took in boarders—distant cousins, usually—to help pay the rent.

I continued to have a hard time in school, not only with my class-mates, but also with my teachers. I remember one particularly pain-ful incident that took place when I was in fourth grade.

I was sitting in class, doing my best to read my book, when I heard fire engines outside. Now, I had never seen a fire engine, not in real life. But shortly before, I'd seen a movie about a fire, in which the firemen, riding their engines, were the heroes. Since I was at an impressionable age, this had stuck in my mind.

Hearing the sirens and the clanging bells, I got excited. I jumped up from my seat and started shouting *i pompieri, i pompieri!* (the firemen, the firemen!). Everyone in the class burst out laughing, and I was ridiculed and shamed.

My teacher, a very vicious person, came over to me with fury in her eyes and a ruler in her hands. "Stick out your hands," she said.

I did. And she whacked me with the ruler with such force that she cut my fingers. I still have the scars—and all because I interrupted the class for a moment.

My first reaction was astonishment. Why would she hit me? The teacher—the priest—sometimes smacked the children in Montorio when we were especially mischievous. But here, in America? It wasn't right.

Mama, with her uncertain command of the language, tried to intercede on my behalf with the school principal. But the principal said, "My teachers don't hit for no reason. If your Costanzo got smacked, it was because he was a bad boy."

When Mama came home, she told me that there was nothing she could do, that I'd just have to take it. So I did. And I decided never again to open my mouth in class. I went into my own world.

That world was one of glamor, excitement, and beauty. It was a world of Hollywood, of the movies, of Valentino. For me, the palace of fantasy was the Paragon Theater, on Fulton Street.

Valentino had died before I arrived in the United States, but his films were still popular in the late 1920s, when I saw them. They were a revelation to me. More than anything, I wanted to be like Valentino—or like Ramon Novarro or Douglas Fairbanks or similar stars. I saw myself in their image.

When I wasn't sitting in the Paragon, gaping at the screen, I was clipping pictures out of movie magazines and pasting them in scrapbooks.

I collected photos of Charles Boyer, Walter Huston, John Gilbert, and all the other famous leading men I wanted to be like. And I also cut out the photos of Mary Pickford, Joan Crawford, Marlene Dietrich, Jeanette MacDonald, Greta Garbo, Nazimova, and the other beautiful women of the day. I still have the scrapbooks.

One day, walking down Rockaway Avenue, near Fulton Street, I happened to pass an Italian pastry shop called "Ariola's." The smells coming out of it were beautiful—and so were the pastries and cakes in the window. I knew sweets weren't for me, but what harm could there be in looking—and sniffing?

Pretty soon, I found myself walking past this pastry shop every day. I even struck up a nodding acquaintance with the lady who sat out in front of the store, minding her baby.

After a few weeks of saying hello, she called me over. "How would you like to have a job?" she asked.

"Me? Doing what?"

"Helping out in the bakery, after school."

"Let me ask my mother."

In my family, all such decisions were handled by Mama. She managed the day-to-day affairs of the family, while my father sat back, the symbol of authority, setting an austere example for us to follow.

Papa was not a man who easily shared his thoughts or feelings, even with his children, yet he was a generous man, a loving husband and father. In a sense, he acted the role of king, while my mother played the part of prime minister.

At any rate, when Mama found out that both the baker, Don Crescenzo Ariola, and his wife were Neapolitans, she quickly approved. Looking back on it now, however, I realize she must have had other reasons for wanting me to take the job.

She must have sensed that it might very well help bring me out of my shell, and at the same time keep me out of trouble. Then, too, there was the money. I'd been offered two dollars a week—not much today, perhaps, but a sizable amount back in 1929 or 1930. Besides, baking was part of my heritage. I'd come from a long line of bakers.

And so I started working at the pastry shop, from about three-thirty in the afternoon until eight-thirty at night on weekdays, and all day Saturday and Sunday. I soon came to love my job and the people I was working for. They felt the same about me, perhaps partly because I never ate any of the sweets.

My specialty in those days was cream puffs. I was convinced I was the best cream puff maker in the world. Even now, I'm sure that the baker was one of the best. He used only first-rate ingredients—the finest flour, the purest vanilla, the ripest lemons, etc. If he found a single flaw in the finished product, he threw it out.

His skills made him one of the busiest caterers in Brooklyn. We were forever making four-foot-high wedding cakes or trayfuls of incredible pastries. Then the baker's other assistant—Tony—and I would deliver them in the baker's van.

I didn't know it at the time, but many of those deliveries were to families whose names are well known today—the Anastasias, the Gambinos, the Lucianos, and their friends and business associates.

And I didn't understand—until later—who that man was who visited the baker's shop every month, who was greeted coldly and unceremoniously given a small envelope.

Least of all did I see the storm clouds approaching in my own life, nor did I dream of the role that Ariola the baker would play when, mainly through innocence, I faced dishonor and destruction.

THREE

As I entered my adolescence, I more and more found that my life was full of problems, threats—and temptations.

My most immediate problem involved school. I just wasn't making it. Though I'd made plenty of friends among my classmates by now, I still wasn't getting along very well with my teachers. As a result, my grades were poor.

After a year in junior high, I wanted very much to quit school, to work, to go out into the world, to get involved with real life somehow, to do anything but sit in a classroom or study.

This attitude triggered a series of shouting matches between Mama and me that must have entertained half of Brooklyn. She'd tell me she not only wanted me to finish public school, but she also wanted me to go to college.

I'd tell her I didn't want any part of school, that I wanted to go out and make my mark. "Someday, someday," I usually ended up shouting, "you'll see what I'm going to do!"

My mother would just shake her head and despair for my future.

My eighth-grade art teacher provided a solution to the problem. He'd been watching my work for some time and had often told me I had unusual artistic skills, especially when it came to design.

Knowing my unhappiness with school, he took me aside one day for a heart-to-heart talk. "Costanzo," he said, "you enter high school next year, right?"

"Right."

"And you're not very happy about it."

"No."

"Well, I have another idea for you. I know of a small art school in

Manhattan with an excellent reputation. There may be a chance you could go there instead of continuing in regular school."

That night, I came home and begged with Mama. And the next day, she went to the school principal and pleaded with him, the art teacher lending his support. The principal took my case to the Board of Education.

Within a few weeks, I had entered Leonardo Da Vinci Art School, on Thirty-fourth Street in Manhattan, between Lexington and Third avenues. And there I began to study design, drawing, painting, architecture, and sculpture.

At this school, I acquired what I'd never had in public school—real friends, boys with whom I shared the same interests, teachers who were genuinely concerned about my progress. I began to go to parties with these friends and join their clubs.

Not only did I learn valuable lessons about design, color, and balance, but I also began to feel a part of something. I began to see a path for myself, a direction in which I could go, a possible future.

Mama still had cause to worry about me, however. My school hours may have been taken care of, but I had plenty of time to get into trouble after school—and plenty of opportunity, considering the neighborhood we lived in. It was the breeding ground for Murder, Inc., and the home turf of the Cosa Nostra.

At first, I wasn't aware of anything unusual. There were some young men on our street who were known to make their living stealing from warehouses. And there was a speakeasy next door to our house. I often went there to buy a pitcher of beer. The whole neighborhood did that. But there was nothing remarkable about this.

Then one evening, after walking a girlfriend home, I walked back to my house only to stumble over this huge, soft thing. It was the body of a dead man. I thought, my God, there must have been a car accident here, or maybe a fight. Then I saw an ice pick sticking out of his back. I ran all the way home.

No sooner had I closed the door behind me than there was a tremendous banging from without. "Open up," a gruff voice yelled. "It's the police!"

I opened the door, quaking, to find a pair of huge, angry cops glaring at me.

"What do you know about that body?"

"Where were you between the hours of 5:00 P.M. and 11:00 P.M.?"

"Can anyone corroborate your story?"

"Why didn't you report the murder to the police?"

"Were you a witness to what happened?"

Thank God it was soon established that I had nothing to do with the entire affair, that I was an innocent in every sense of the word, which I truly was.

Almost before I knew it, my innocence nearly got me into trouble again. I found an attractive girl at school and started taking her out to movies or for ice cream sodas.

On one occasion, we happened to bump into one of the older boys in the neighborhood, a kid who lived a few doors away from us. The next day, he made a point of seeking me out.

"Hey, Gus," he said (everyone called me Gus in those days—it was a diminutive of Costanzo), "I see you're going out with Susie. You'd better watch yourself, you know."

"What do you mean? She's a nice girl."

"Maybe so, but she's someone else's girl. Someone important."

Now I got up on my high horse. "Well, who cares about that? If that's true, she'll tell me. I don't have to hear it from you."

But a few days later, I heard the same thing from another friend. So I looked up the girl. "What's going on with you?" I asked her. "I keep hearing stories about another guy."

I'd been drawn to the girl because she was older and more sophisticated than I. She was a bleached blonde with an incredibly bright smile and drawers full of tight sweaters.

Now she looked at me with her most provocative look. "Well," she said, "I have a friend and I've been going out with him here and there. To be perfectly honest, I've been sleeping with him."

I was about fourteen at this time, and a young fourteen at that. If this was an invitation, I didn't understand it. Such talk was way over my head. "Maybe we'd better stop seeing each other, then," I managed. She didn't protest.

Her body was found in a trunk a few months later. I guess she'd had *two* other boyfriends. Perhaps both of them were important—or they thought they were.

Mama was very unhappy about all of this, of course. She knew I was a good boy, that I wouldn't purposely do anything wrong. But she worried plenty. She was afraid I'd fall in with the neighborhood hoodlums.

At the time, though, she was preoccupied with my sister Norina.

Norina had decided to become an actress, and she'd joined a sleazy, fly-by-night acting school.

While at school, she happened to meet a Sicilian shoemaker who fancied himself a dancer. He wanted to put a vaudeville act together, with a South American flavor. I don't know why.

Well, after weeks of sweet-talking her and my Mama, sometimes at our house, Norina was convinced. She began taking lessons in Spanish dance from Madame Helen Veola, who had a studio on Fifty-ninth Street in Manhattan, between Fifth and Madison avenues, around the corner from the Sherry-Netherland Hotel.

My sister went to Madame Veola's studio two or three evenings a week, always chaperoned by my mother. During these trips, my mother learned everything there was to learn about Broadway. She eventually learned about studios, about rehearsals, about vaudeville and legitimate theater, about Carnegie Hall, Town Hall, and the Metropolitan Opera.

And I, as usual, was getting myself into trouble again, quite innocently. At this time, we were living on Somers Street. Our backyard, we soon discovered, faced the backyard of a photographer—the same man who'd taken our family pictures!

I quite naturally became friends with his son—I think his name was Paul—who was two or three years younger than I. We started having snacks at his house after school.

"Why don't you stay for a while," his father suggested one afternoon. "I'll show you some beautiful photographs I took of a wedding the other day."

So I stayed. He had his assistant—a not unattractive young woman of nineteen or twenty—bring out the pictures. And I enjoyed looking at them.

Two or three days later, Paul and I were at his house again. The photographer sent his son off on an errand and again offered to show me some pictures. Why not? I thought. Maybe he wants to teach me. Maybe he's looking for another assistant.

The first few pictures in the pile were typical wedding pictures. Then, suddenly, I came across a photo of a naked young girl, then more, and still more, from every possible angle. My imagination was provoked, of course. I looked. I enjoyed looking.

"Pretty, isn't she?"

"She sure is."

"You can have her if you want."

I didn't get the message. "I think I know this girl," I said. "Doesn't she live in the neighborhood?"

"I don't think you know her," he said.

Nothing more happened that day. But I had strange feelings about what had occurred. This mature man was fostering some kind of mysterious association between himself and me. It was all beyond my comprehension.

A few days later, my mother asked me to go to the photographer's. She wanted some copies of the first pictures he'd taken of our family. When I went in, there was no one downstairs. So I went right upstairs, since I'd been there before.

I called for the photographer, then for his son—but no one answered. Then I called for the photographer's wife.

"Yes," she said. "I'm in here, in the bedroom."

When I walked into the room, I found her in bed with the photographer's assistant, the young girl.

"It's four in the afternoon," I said. "Are you sick?" I could see she wasn't sick.

She smiled.

"Well, maybe I'd better come back later."

I left the house and tried to put the matter out of my mind.

By the time I saw the photographer again, several months later, I'd pretty much forgotten what I'd seen at his house. After all, it had made no sense to me.

The photographer was very friendly toward me. "You know, I've sent Paul to summer camp."

"That sounds nice."

"It is. Very nice. You'd really like it. Tell you what: Why don't you go there for a week—my treat. I know Paul would enjoy your company."

Mama, who had no reason to suspect the photographer was anything other than a friendly neighbor, said fine.

The place I went to was a beautiful farm in upstate New York, with a lake and horses and all kinds of outdoor things to do. Paul and I and the farmer's two daughters had a great time.

After I'd been there three or four days, I saw a familiar car drive through the gate. It was, of all people, the baker—the pastry man!

"Gus!" he said, his face grim. "Is the photographer here yet?"

"He brought us here, then he left. But I don't understand. Why are you here? What's wrong?"

He ignored my confusion. "What about the girl? Is she here?"

"There's no girl—only the farmer's daughters. What's this all about?" I was mystified.

"Come on, I'm taking you home. Right now."

"But why?"

"Just come with me. If you don't, you'll regret it for the rest of your life."

Well, I respected the baker. I trusted him. He'd never done anything concerning me that wasn't for my benefit. So I threw my things into my suitcase, said good-bye to everyone, and drove off with him.

On the way home, he told me that the police suspected the photographer of being a child molester or a rapist. It was thought he'd gotten a young girl pregnant and that he was going to try to involve me with her to save himself.

Evidently, the pastrymaker had heard my name mentioned along with the girl's and the photographer's. He was sure that none of this was my work, that the photographer must be behind it all. Somehow, he found out where I was and rescued me.

Eventually, the photographer was arrested and convicted. I think he got eight years in jail. The girl was put into an institution. She turned out to be the girl whose pictures the photographer had shown me that day at his house.

Mama was sure I was involved, one way or another. She's one of those people who feels that where there's smoke, there's fire. And in my case, there had been a great deal of smoke.

She gave me the beating of my life, despite my protestations, despite the fact that no one was accusing me of anything. Then, to make sure I didn't get into any more trouble, either of my own making or through bad associations, she told me I was to chaperone my sister to Madame Veola's from then on. That way, I just wouldn't have time for mischief.

I couldn't have guessed it then, but Mama's order—born out of caring and concern—would turn out to be one of the key events in my life.

FOUR

After a while, it all fell into a routine. Every Monday and Wednesday evening and every Saturday afternoon, I'd accompany Norina to her dancing class at Madame Veola's studio. Every Tuesday night, we'd come to see recitals by some of her most accomplished students or other famous performers.

In her day, Madame Veola was probably the best teacher of Spanish dance in New York. In some ways, the art she taught wasn't as authentic as that of certain other dance instructors, but she made up for that with her high standards and her extremely progressive method of teaching.

Besides, she was a great lady of dance, respected and admired by all. And her actor husband, who frequently came to the studio, was a true gentleman and a genuine inspiration to his wife's students.

While my sister learned, I sat and watched, fascinated. I partook not only of the lessons, but also of the atmosphere. I got to know the other students. I met the dance aficionados who attended the recitals, and I watched the famous performers with awe.

Very often, I'd be at home while my sister practiced her steps to a record. Like any brother, I couldn't resist teasing her. "You're no good," I'd say with a gleam in my eye. "You're stupid. I'm not a dancer, but I know the steps better than you do."

Norina finally rose to the bait, her cheeks coloring. "Is that so?" she said. "Well, if you think you're so smart, why don't you show me."

"Okay," I said, smiling, "I will."

And I got up and did the routine she'd been practicing. Only I did it perfectly, move for move, step for step. Where she'd faltered, I had no trouble. Where she'd been unsure of herself, I was steady and confident.

After about a month of this brother-sister teasing, Norina got so exasperated that she mentioned my antics to Madame Veola, in front of the whole class. "You know, he makes my life miserable at home," she said. "He says he's a better dancer than I am."

Madame Veola had always taken a friendly interest in me, asking me how I was doing in art school, inquiring after my mother, etc. Now she was intrigued by my sister's remark.

"Are you really a good dancer, Costanzo?"

I smiled nervously. The whole class was looking on, including a pretty girl I'd been trying to flirt with. "I don't know."

"Your sister says you think you're a good dancer. Will you show us?"

"Show you?"

The girl was watching me, waiting to see if I were going to make a fool of myself.

"Yes. Let me put on the music. Then you can show us."

There was no way out. When the record began, I took my place on the floor and started to dance. I put everything I had into it. I was determined not to shame myself.

When I finished, the entire class broke out into applause. I was flabbergasted. But Madame Veola looked reserved and serious. "Costanzo," she said, "please tell your mother to come in and talk to me. You have a great talent. We must not let it go to waste."

A great talent. Wonderful words to hear, of course, but what did they really mean to me? It was 1933. I was a few months short of being fifteen years old. I was midway between being a boy and a young man.

When I told Mama what Madame Veola had said, she despaired of being able to pay my tuition at the studio, in addition to my sister's. Not only was it the middle of the Depression, but also my father had suddenly come down with a severe case of arthritis.

His hands were so affected he was unable to work. Mama was supporting the family with piecework from the garment district.

But Madame Veola was determined that these circumstances not prevent me from studying dance. She saw to it that I got a scholarship. And so I began to learn the art that was to provide me with meaning and sustenance for the rest of my life.

Soon after I began dancing school, my education at Leonardo Da

Vinci Art School came to an end. Partly through the support of Fiorello LaGuardia, the school had managed to survive the first couple of years after the crash. But it finally ran out of funds and closed.

I went to work, at the Atlas Ticket Agency, on Forty-fourth Street Broadway, as a runner. From about ten in the morning until eight at night, I delivered theater tickets all over the city.

And I began to learn, as Mama had learned a few years earlier, the difference between Broadway and the Palace, what the Shubert Theater was, who Lee Shubert and Sol Hurok were.

I was enchanted with the world of theater and show business. Whenever I wasn't dancing, I'd manage to get a ticket or two to the latest hit—*Porgy and Bess, Abe Lincoln in Illinois, Dead End, Golden Boy, The Iceman Cometh*. I saw all the great dramatic productions of the day.

I also saw and worshiped from a distance the great dramatic stars of that age: Ina Claire, Raymond Massey, Paul Muni, Ethel Barrymore, Noël Coward, and all the rest, and the great comedy stars, Bert Lahr and Ed Wynn, and the great musical stars, Ethel Merman, Paul Haakon, and others.

And I never missed any of the great spectacles of the era—the great *Ziegfeld Follies, Earl Carroll's Vanities,* and *George White's Scandals.*

In a way, as a ticket runner, I was part of it. I hovered around the edges of show business. But I wanted more. I wanted to be on the inside. At the time, it seemed a futile gesture—so I watched.

I don't think I really realized it then, but I was doing more than just watching. I was absorbing. I was learning about lighting, costuming, pathos, humor. I was learning the difference between a lackluster production and a sensational one.

Every so often, while hanging around the Atlas Ticket Agency, I'd meet some minor show business figure. My pitch was always the same: "I'm studying Spanish dancing. I may be one of the best Spanish dancers in the world. Can you do anything for me?"

And the answer was almost always the same: "Spanish dancer? They're a dime a dozen. The night clubs and casinos are full of them. Why don't you learn to be like Fred Astaire?"

"Well, I don't know how to tap. I do everything on the heel, he does everything on the toe."

The person I was talking to would then smile and shrug and say something like, "Sorry, kid. Wish I could help."

23

I remember one occasion of this sort quite vividly. Through a friend at Madame Veola's, I met a man named John Nonnenbacher. Nonnenbacher had been the managing director of Baron Singer's Midgets—the great troupe of tiny singers, dancers, and circus performers who eventually became the Munchkins in the *Wizard of Oz* movie.

More recently, he'd taken on the management of Paul Haakon, a Danish ballet dancer. He'd taken Haakon out of his ballet company and had started building him into a top Broadway attraction. I hoped that by some miracle, he might do the same for me.

I made an appointment to see Mr. Nonnenbacher at his Broadway office, next to the Loew's State Theater building. There, I explained my ambitions. Nonnenbacher was a chubby-faced, balding man with twinkling eyes and a big grin. He listened to me with a friendly expression.

When I finished, he shook his head sadly. "Listen, Greco," he said, "the trouble with Spanish dancers is that they're a dime a dozen. Do yourself a favor and take my advice. Get a good, steady job. Learn how to drive a truck or something. Forget this Spanish dancing."

I left his office with tears in my eyes. I wasn't about to give up my dancing. I'd hardly even begun. What's more—though I couldn't have known it—my first success was just around the corner.

It's gone now, but once there was a great theater on Sixth Avenue in New York known as the Hippodrome. In those days, it was rented by a man named Salmaggi, an opera impresario. He used it to present operas at a popular price—a dollar for a choice seat, vs. five or six at the Met.

I was practicing at Madame Veola's one afternoon when Salmaggi's ballet mistress paid a call. She was looking for dancers. As fate would have it, her eye fell on me.

"Oh, I don't think his mother would approve," Madame Veola said. "She doesn't want him to get into show business."

That was true enough. She felt one child in show business—Norina—was enough. But getting into show business was *my* fondest hope. I managed to convince Mama that dancing in an opera wouldn't do me any permanent damage.

The ballet mistress decided she wanted me to do a solo dance—with a female partner—in the opera *La Traviata*. She wanted me for the party scene, in which Traviata introduces her lover to her society friends.

Madame Veola picked out a petite, dark, Spanish-looking girl (of French parentage, it happened) she thought would be a suitable partner—a young woman in her early twenties named Fifi. And we began to rehearse. We rehearsed for weeks.

It was the first time in my life, really, that I'd spent so much time with one girl. By this time, I was approaching seventeen. I knew what boys and girls could do together. I'd heard all about it from my friends at the ticket agency.

Those friends were always talking about this girl or that girl, what she would do or what she wouldn't do. Also, one of them had visited Havana and had brought back some pornographic pictures.

Things like that prey on the mind. Like any young man, I was anything but immune. Soon, I began to have thoughts about Fifi. I realized she might be more than just a dancing partner.

Someone told me about this place in the Fifties that, for a few dollars, offered real privacy. That evening, after rehearsal, I invited Fifi to dinner, then suggested that we go to this place for coffee. I was really nervous. I showed too much anxiety, I suppose, and no experience whatsoever.

Although Fifi knew more about such things than I did, she was timid. And before I realized it, it was all over. Everything went wrong. I knew that. But I behaved as a gentleman should. I showed her kindness and tried to make her laugh—which she did.

But I knew, even then, that we were all finished as lovers. Oh, we continued to dance together for a few performances, but we weren't anything more than dance partners.

A few days later, a huge audience gave us prolonged applause after one of our performances. We took our bows; then, to my amazement, Fifi immediately left the stage and went into the wings. I stood there, still overcome by the audience's reaction, not knowing what to do. I couldn't move. I stood rooted to the stage, unable to walk off.

"Hey, you," the tenor hissed, "get off the stage."

My legs wouldn't start walking.

"You're finished. Your bit is over. Scram!"

I stared at him with glazed eyes.

"Get off the damn stage, dummy!"

25

He gave me a yank that wrenched me out of my reverie. As I scurried into the wings, I could hear the music begin again. Then the tenor started singing. But the applause was still ringing in my ears. I loved it. I've never stopped loving it.

They gave Fifi and me six dollars each for that show. And a few nights later, we collected another six dollars for doing a similar dance in *Carmen*.

While taking classes at Madame Veola's, a new girl soon attracted my attention, a slender, almond-eyed brunette from Puerto Rico. Her name was Sarita.

Sarita had a perfect face, with haunting, bewitching eyes. She carried herself like a regal Spanish lady, radiating dignity, class, warmth, and passion.

Oh, I really fell for her.

Through her, I met her cousin, Joaquin (hwa-keen), a fascinating, gnomelike little man who was full of interesting opinions and ideas. He became my close link to Sarita.

Before long, I was very much in love with her, or so I thought. I would look for any excuse to dance near her or with her or go out together with her and Joaquin after class.

Often we'd go to Child's Spanish Garden, on Fifty-ninth Street. What a beautiful place that was. It had a wonderful marimba band that played tangos, rhumbas, and boleros.

It was during these outings that I became aware of Sarita's Puerto Rican origins. Like any lovesick young man might have done, I read all I could about the island, about its geographical location, its topography, its climate, its flora and fauna.

When I learned how heavenly the island was, I felt it was only natural that it should be my beautiful Sarita's homeland. Somehow, my knowledge of Puerto Rico increased my love for her. And it stimulated a desire in me to learn the Spanish language. With Sarita's help, that's what I did.

Meanwhile, Joaquin and I became close friends. I often invited him to my house to dinner. Mama and Norina also became fond of him, I think partly because he so obviously thought highly of me.

Very often, Joaquin entertained us at the piano—and he was a remarkable pianist. He also talked about the great dancers, singers, and musicians he had seen and admired—people like Argentina, Escudero, Brailovsky, Pavlova, Kurtzberg, Rubinstein, and other untouchable stars. How vividly he brought them to life, how much he excited my imagination! I could almost see them perform as he talked about them.

In bringing these artists alive to me and to my family, Joaquin demonstrated something else: He, too, was a vivid artist, in his own special way.

As my friendship with Joaquin grew, so did my relationship with Sarita. Little by little, I began to speak endearing words to her. And she seemed to share my feelings.

What was happening between us was soon obvious to all. Our feelings for each other were reflected in the way we danced together. For that reason, our duets—whether flamenco or tango—at Madame Veola's Tuesday night recitals quickly became the highlight of the evening.

Eventually, lost in a cloud of love, we married. It didn't matter to me that I was still in my teens, or that Sarita was five or six years older than I.

It was still a rough road for me when it came to passionate fulfillment, but I was learning. So was Sarita. Though we were both terribly young and inexperienced, we tried to build a relationship together. She tried more than I, I think.

But it was not to be. Sarita, of course, loved me dearly. But she was not "in love" with me, however much she wanted to be. After a short time, she left me.

FIVE

I was devastated by Sarita's rejection. I cried until I thought I'd used up my life's supply of tears. I began to understand what pathos really was.

At the time, I loved her dearly, though now it seems to me that my main reason for marrying her might have been to make love to her.

But I remember taking the whole thing very hard at the time—so hard, in fact, that I felt I had to change my life in some dramatic way, that I couldn't continue at Madame Veola's or with my job at the ticket agency.

Through some friends in our neighborhood, I heard that if you paid a certain man fifty dollars, he would get you a job at the Ford Motor Company in Detroit, on the production line. That was the kind of change I thought I wanted to make. I scraped up the money, made the payoff, and then left for Detroit, with a couple of other fellows.

We got there, rented a shabby furnished room, and waited to be summoned to work. We waited around for six months, but the summons never came. The payoff scheme was a racket, nothing more. I'd been a sucker.

While I waited, I had to earn money somehow, at least enough to pay for my share of the room and for food. So I got a job washing dishes at Detroit's Masonic Temple.

At the time, this was one of the city's most outstanding halls. It was the site not only of all kinds of industrial exhibits, but also where many top concert performers played.

I remember looking longingly at their posters as I came and went.

There were pictures of Marian Anderson, Yehudi Menuhin, Andres Segovia, Arthur Rubinstein, and similar stars.

While they played to fancy audiences upstairs, I washed dishes downstairs for some convention or other. Sometimes, applause reverberated throughout the building. I was miserable.

After I left New York, I heard that Sarita had joined a traveling circus. One of our mutual friends wrote me and told me that Sarita's circus was going to play Toledo, Ohio—about an hour's drive from Detroit. I was determined to see her, to convince her to change her mind.

With a friend, I drove to Toledo and we found the circus. I searched out Sarita and began to plead with her. I told her how much I longed for her, how much I loved her, how much I wanted to make love to her—right there and then, if possible.

She wasn't happy to see me. She refused all my overtures. When the time came for her to perform, she was only too happy to leave. I went back to my furnished room in Detroit, feeling empty.

A few days later, I got a letter from Sarita. She didn't feel we should stay married. She wanted a divorce. Eventually, she took the necessary legal steps, and that was that.

Finally, I realized that I was never going to have a chance to build automobiles for Ford. My economic state was precarious, and my emotional state was even worse. I returned to New York, to our home on Fifty-sixth Street, in Manhattan. There was no place else to go.

I also returned to the Atlas Ticket Agency and to Madame Veola's. Maybe I couldn't make cars, but I could still dance. And I was still a year or so short of twenty. Perhaps I had a future, regardless of Sarita.

Everyone was happy to have me back—Madame Veola, the Atlas brothers (owners of the ticket agency), Joaquin and my other friends, and, of course, my family. My return eased the financial burden on Mama, who'd been sending me money to help sustain me in Detroit.

Not long before, my sister Norina had made her own debut at Salmaggi's popularly priced opera—as a singer. Ironically, she first performed in the same opera in which—a year and a half or two years earlier—I'd made my debut: *Traviata*. Now she was appearing with various small opera companies, sometimes touring with them. Her career looked promising indeed.

Not mine, though.

Maybe I hadn't been serious enough about my dancing in the past. I don't know. Anyhow, when I returned to Madame Veola's, I took on a little more professional attitude. I knew I could never support myself as a ticket runner. My best hope lay in dancing.

At dancing class, I met Muriel Bentley, who later became a very well-known dancer and now runs an actors' booking agency in New York. I also met and became friends with other now-famous dancers, such as Nora Kaye and Jerome Robbins. Muriel and I began to dance together, as a team. Again, I found myself performing at Salmaggi's operas and—every now and then—at supper clubs.

It wasn't enough for me. I wanted more work. I wanted a career. It seemed to me that if I stayed at Madame Veola's, that would never happen. It had a congenial atmosphere, but it didn't seem to be leading anywhere.

If I were going to be a Spanish dancer, I decided, mabe I'd better find a Spaniard to teach me. A truly Spanish teacher might also have better professional contacts.

So I began to study with Aurora Arriaza, a Spaniard with extensive acquaintances among other Spanish people in New York. She had been the dancing partner of a famous Argentinian ballroom dancer in the early and mid-1930s.

I stayed with this Spanish lady for about a year, during which time I teamed up with another girl, one who had all kinds of connections. Together, we performed at many supper clubs, night clubs, country clubs, etc., in New York and other nearby cities. I wasn't making a fortune, but I was dancing professionally.

I also began to meet other professional Spanish dancers and a number of nondancers who were either Spanish or who were immersed in Spanish culture. We often talked about Spain and about the best Spanish dancers.

We discussed Carmen Amaya, perhaps the greatest flamenco soloist who ever lived or ever will live. We also talked, with awe, of Spain's greatest male dancer, Vicente Escudero, the personification of elegance and masculinity.

We went on and on about a woman named Argentina, who'd died a couple of years earlier. She was the person largely responsible for resurrecting Spain's traditional dances and joining them with the music of Albeniz, Turina, Granados, De Falla, and others.

We also talked about her legendary successor and heir, the fantastic Argentinita, the toast of Spain, companion to Ignacio Sanchez Mejias—one of Spain's greatest bullfighters, friend to Garcia Lorca, Edgar Neville, and many other philosophers, poets, and politicians.

As it happened, Argentinita often performed in New York in those days, under the auspices of Sol Hurok. On at least two occasions that I can recall, I sat in the audience and watched her, astounded by the lyrical femininity she brought to her art.

At the time, Argentinita's partner was a man from Seville named Antonio Triana. He, too, impressed me—so much so that when I heard he was willing to give private lessons, I jumped at the opportunity.

I arranged to begin with him and pay him as I learned. This seemed to suit him well enough. We worked together for about a week. He was friendly enough at the start, but he grew colder with each passing day.

At first, I thought it was because I wasn't catching on quickly enough. I tried harder. This apparently made him even angrier. Finally, at the end of the week, there was a confrontation.

"I want my money now," he said bluntly.

"Now? I thought I could pay you at the end of the month."

"I want it now. You learn too fast. I won't have anything more to teach you by that time."

It was a wonderful compliment, but it gave me a horrible problem. I didn't have the money, and I didn't know where to get it. I don't remember the amount anymore. Perhaps it was a hundred dollars. Certainly Mama didn't have it.

The person who came to my rescue was my shy, ugly, and devoted friend Joaquin. He advanced me the money willingly, gladly, with love. How could I reject his offer?

How Joaquin got the money, I never found out. He was nearly as poor as I. But he had a job and he knew how to finagle things—not always honestly, either.

He was in charge of the mail room of a large corporation. Among other things, it was his job to buy the stamps. Every so often, he'd come to me with a few sheets of stamps and give them to me.

"What do I need with all these stamps, Joaquin? How many letters do you think I write?"

"Go down to such-and-such a street and see a man named so-and-so. He'll buy those stamps from you at ninety-nine cents on the dollar."

I argued with him that this was wrong, but he wouldn't be convinced. He told me that his employers mistreated and underpaid him and this was his way of getting back at them.

I refused to take the stamps, but he wouldn't take "No" for an answer. He cajoled me into meeting him right after he sold the stamps. We took the proceeds and went to a local car dealer, where each of us made down payments on an automobile. It was my first and, I admit, it made me feel like a king.

Joaquin's stamp trick helped with the installments, too. But finally, the whole thing began to prey on my mind. I felt that the car would be bad luck, that I might have an accident in it.

I ended up selling the car—and buying another. I didn't give the money back, but I didn't take any more, either. Thank God, Joaquin never got caught.

While I'd been trying to establish myself as a Spanish dancer, with no particular success, Norina's career blossomed. She'd been discovered by the Met. She was now singing leading rolls in *Aïda*, *Il Trovatore*, and other operas, opposite such first-rank stars as Lawrence Tibbett.

Critics thought Norina had a wonderful voice and stage presence. They called her the most exciting newcomer to appear in years, someone bound to challenge the more established divas, comparing her favorably to Rosa Ponselle, another famous soprano.

After my experience with Señor Triano, the dance teacher, I decided to go back "home," to return to Madame Veola. She'd been hurt when I left, and I wanted to regain her friendship. We were *simpático*, and that was something I just couldn't sacrifice.

While having lunch one day at a hot dog stand, on the way to her studio, I looked up to find a familiar face gazing at me.

"Greco, isn't it? Costanzo Greco?"

"Yes."

"I'm John Nonnenbacher—Jack. I remember talking to you in my office."

"Oh, yes," I said. "You thought I had a talent for truck driving."

He shrugged in an ingratiating, self-deprecating gesture. "Maybe I was wrong. What do I know? How are you doing?"

"I'm still a Spanish dancer. I haven't set the world on fire yet, but I'm making a few bucks."

"That's good. And how's that sister of yours?"

"She stopped dancing and took up singing. She's at the Met now, doing very well."

"At the Met? Is her name Norina, Norina Greco?"

"That's my sister."

"That's amazing. I hear her practicing all the time."

This made no sense to me. "What do you mean?"

"Well, I hear her voice coming into the window of my apartment almost every day."

We soon established that we were neighbors—we lived on Fifty-sixth Street, he lived on Fifty-fifth. Our backyards abutted. Before I knew it, Jack and I were friends.

He wasn't in a position to help me professionally at that time, but he did give me valuable advice and support. And his sense of humor kept us all in stitches, even when things were at their worst.

At Madame Veola's studio, I had a hard time forgetting Sarita. My memories of her made it very hard for me. I tried putting even more into my dancing. I finally thought I'd found a new partner, a tall, Irish-Italian girl with a wide smile named Teresa. She and I teamed up and, together, we found more club jobs than ever before.

I was pleased to be supporting myself, or at least contributing my fair share to the family finances. But Teresa was more ambitious. She wanted to audition for the more pretentious spots.

One day, she came to me and excitedly told me her sister Meda was returning from Texas.

"That's nice," I said, not much interested.

"Don't you remember?" She asked. "Meda was one of the original Rockettes. She went to Texas to appear in Billy Rose's *Casa Mañana*. She's a wonderful pianist."

"I see." I didn't see.

"She can help us in rehearsals. And she can go with us on auditions. She's just what we need."

"Well, maybe so," I said. I thought no more about it.

I was attending one of Madame Veola's Tuesday evening recitals a few weeks later when I noticed a girl I'd never seen before in the audience. I stared at her. Anyone would have stared at her. She was beautiful. At least she seemed so to me.

As she sat there watching quietly, wearing a little blue beret, I looked at her. She was slender and pale, with exquisitely delicate features. Yet there was a provocative, seductive aspect to her.

33

Above all, she was mysterious, not unlike Nazimova or Nita Naldi, of the silent movie era. Who was this beautiful girl? For that matter, why was she having such an impact on me?

After recital, Teresa brought her over to me.

"This is my sister Meda," she said.

"Hello."

I was obsessed with her. I was used to warm, outgoing people. Here was a soft, quiet girl—no, not a girl, a woman. I saw depths in her that I'd seen in no one else.

In the days that followed, I saw a lot of Meda, usually at Teresa's home. Meda would play the piano for us and for other dancers who were studying with Madame Veola. Then we'd all sit down to pasta and meatballs.

But I never approached Meda. I thought she was far, far above me.

I guess I'd known her a month or so when one of the Atlas brothers—from the ticket agency—invited a bunch of Madame Veola's students to a party at his Riverside Drive apartment.

I drove up from Brooklyn—we'd moved again—in my car. It wasn't the one I'd bought with the stamps, but its successor, a beautiful LaSalle. We had a wonderful dinner at the Atlas's, then we got up, with the thought of continuing the party elsewhere, perhaps.

Meda approached me. "Are you going home alone? Or are you taking someone?"

"I'm going alone."

"Oh, good. Maybe you could take me home. I'd like to get there before my sister does."

Meda lived in Coney Island, not far from my house. "Sure," I said, "why not?"

We left the party, got into the LaSalle, and zoomed off. As we drove toward Brooklyn, we began to talk, about dance, about music, about her life and mine.

As we approached her neighborhood, she said, "Don't go down my street. Just pull off here, so we can talk for a while."

"Well, all right, fine," I said. I stopped the car on this very dark street.

"Do you know that I dreamed about you last night and I owe you a quarter?"

"What does that mean?"

"If you don't know what that means, you're an idiot."

"Well, I'm an idiot, then."

For a moment, she said nothing. Then she smiled at me, almost shyly, and she said very softly, "It means I want you to love me."

SIX

I looked at Meda and I saw an angel. This incredible woman wanted me to make love to her. Being of sound mind and body, I accepted her invitation with all my heart, with a passion I made no effort to disguise. What followed was the most incredible sexual experience of my life.

We made love for hours, I with a capacity I'd never dreamed I had, she with an earthy womanliness unlike anything I'd ever known. She was the most perfect woman I'd ever met—and she wanted me!

In the months that followed, we had an affair of almost unbearable intensity. That night's experience was repeated again and again —not because I was such a great lover, but because Meda's passion burned with astonishing brightness.

I dreamed about Meda. I thought about her during almost every waking moment. I spent as much time with her as I possibly could, making love, talking, taking her to shows and concerts. I was irretrievably in love, for the first time in my life.

Meda, however, was in a different state. She'd had a horrible experience in Texas, falling in love with a man whose wife refused to give him a divorce.

When I met her, she was convalescing from this unhappy incident. She was hurt. She drank too much, and her sadness possessed her. Sometimes she seemed to be in a trance, and I could not reach her. When these moments occurred, I felt helpless—yet filled with love.

So, at first, Meda was not really in love with me.

But that didn't matter to me. I was overjoyed when she smiled at me, when she touched me on the cheek, when she encouraged me to take her into my arms and join with her.

I passed my twentieth birthday still a boy, but Meda was beginning to change all that. Day after day, week after week, we talked—usually hours at a time. And during this period, she taught me what manhood meant, what life was all about.

Meda shared her life with me, not just her present, but also her past. She told me about her mother, her father, her friends, her tragedies, and her triumphs. She taught me her philosophy of life.

More than that, she talked to me about my life—about my family and friends, about my career. Bit by bit, she taught me how to live, how to behave, how to look at life with serenity, with dignity, how to conduct myself with finesse and pride.

Meda was only four or five years older than I, but she might well have been decades more mature. She had the emotional capacity to experience life to its fullest and the mental ability to comprehend what was going on around her and where she fit in.

In nearly every area of life, Meda was more sophisticated than I. I learned from her just by associating with her, over a two- or three-year period. Most of the time, I was only dimly aware that I was learning. But I was hungry for her companionship and all that it represented, passionately, emotionally, and intellectually.

Meda taught me so many things. She taught me small things about clothes and about the different fragrances of flowers and perfume. She taught me about music and literature. She taught me the ways in which two people can relate to each other.

She even taught me about my own art, for she was a highly talented choreographer, with a vast knowledge of dance and the theater. She had worked with great musicians, great directors, great designers.

She knew that the dance was inspired by birds, by stallions, by fillies, by panthers, even by flowers. She realized that dance movements came from these and other living beings.

She'd gotten her experience in one of the theater's finest ages, in a period filled with spectacularly produced musicals and operettas, when the economics of the day made possible countless lavish shows.

These experiences, this knowledge, she also shared with me. Through her, I learned the elements of pacing, I began to understand the basic components of choreography, I started to grasp the need for projection and the way to accomplish it.

37

In a certain sense, Meda took the boy she found and made him into a man—physically, emotionally, and even artistically. She opened up a thousand doors for me, showed me worlds I'd never dreamed existed. She was one of the most positive, most constructive influences in my life. Obviously, I feel that way even now.

What she transmitted to me in the years we spent together has helped me in my work, in my behavior toward others, in my attitude toward life, in my ability—however large or small it may be—to achieve serenity. She was an extraordinary woman.

Together, we went to Radio City Music Hall and saw Vicente Escudero in a ballet called *Love, the Sorcerer*. In his day, Escudero had no serious rivals. He was unbelievable. He left a profound impression on me and inspired me to greater things.

A few weeks later, I was practicing at Madame Veola's with Teresa and Meda, among others, when a sudden flurry of excitement passed through the room. A distinguished guest was coming. He would arrive momentarily. He was none other than Escudero himself, coming to pay his respects to Madame Veola and to "inspect the troops," so to speak.

I remember him walking through the door, an elegant figure with a great deal of personal magnetism, a man who radiated virility—though he was already in his fifties.

"Will some of your students dance for me?" he asked Madame Veola. My teacher smiled at me and nodded. I swallowed hard, honored at being chosen, anxious to make an impression, or at least to demonstrate competence. Then the music began.

I danced as well as I knew how, my mind buzzing with what I'd learned from Madame Veola, Aurora Arriaza, Antonio Triano—and Meda. I danced my heart out.

When I stopped, Escudero simply gazed at me in silence for a few moments. Everyone held his breath, waiting for some word of praise or disapproval.

Finally, he spoke:

"If I had danced like you do when I was your age," he said, "today I would be the sensation of the world."

Escudero's praise was almost too much for me to absorb. I thanked him as best I could and tried to keep my equilibrium. But I felt proud. And Madame Veola—and Meda—shared my pride.

It was about this time that we heard that Carmen Amaya was coming to town, sponsored—like Argentinita—by Sol Hurok. She was to play at the Beachcomber, next to the Wintergarden Theater, at the present site of the Hawaii Kai Restaurant.

Tickets to her opening were twenty dollars each. I didn't have that kind of money, but I desperately wanted to take Meda to see this famous Spanish dancer. I remember hocking something—a watch, perhaps—to come up with the price of admission.

Meda and I sat there, drinking rum zombies (the cost included two drinks) and watching the famous Carmen Amaya. This incredible dancer was the same age I was, but she'd already made a name for herself throughout Europe.

Carmen Amaya was born a gypsy. She was a true child of the "bronze-skinned folk." She learned to sing and dance just as other children learn to walk and talk. Her father had been a famous flamenco guitarist.

Now, with her two sisters—and her guitarist brother and the now-famous Sabicas—she did her dances for us. Her repertoire was sadly lacking—she did only two dances. But these were the most astounding dances we'd ever seen, more intoxicating, even, than the zombies we were drinking. She was Queen of the Gypsies and of the flamenco.

Carmen Amaya was not physically attractive. But while she was performing, she was beautiful and passionate almost beyond belief. Also, she had enormous technical capacity. Never have I seen anyone heel tap with such intensity, with so much speed. Later I used this sort of thing in my own shows, but I was never able to equal her skill.

So remarkable was her performance and her personality that she completely captivated her audience. But with her limited repertoire, she was never able to find the proper showcase for her talents—she fit comfortably neither into night clubs nor theaters nor concert halls. This unfortunately limited her popularity in the United States.

Eventually she learned something about showmanship and production, following my pattern, and finally achieved undisputed recognition, not only throughout the rest of the world, but also in the United States.

That night at the Beachcomber was magical. And, as I remember, there were other performers in the audience—one in particular, who was to follow Carmen Amaya's engagement: a young newcomer I had seen a year before, with Tommy Dorsey's orchestra in Providence—none other than Frank Sinatra.

Also, there was Boris Karloff, so elegant and British and so unlike the film images he created. And Dorothy Lamour—how lovely she looked.

Later, Meda and I also saw another Spanish dancer, the great Argentinita, the most fully developed Spanish dancer of her time, who had a repertoire that included dances from every part of Spain and expressed humor, pathos, and everything between.

Argentinita was not essentially a solo performer (unlike Carmen Amaya). She had a company of performers—a dozen or more. She performed in theaters and on concert stages, giving an hour-and-a-half show.

While I went with Meda, I danced with several different partners and did a number of club dates. One of these partners was a girl named Gloria Belmonte. When I danced with her, I called myself Ray Serrano.

For a time, we played at Jack Harris's La Conga, on Fifty-first Street and Broadway. *Billboard*, reviewing our performance, said we were a "Spanish team of good technicians working with castanets. Okay for atmosphere"—mild praise indeed.

I also went to Baltimore, where I performed in the Stardust Revue, a big show that Meda choreographed. "A sockaroo solo dance in flamenco style by Costanzo Greco built up to a big showgirl parade," a reviewer said.

In addition, I went to Boston and performed at Ruby Foo's, and to Chicago, where I performed at the Rumba Casino.

At one point, I rehearsed with a girl named Anita Sevilla, a former member of Argentinita's company who'd played with her in South America. I didn't know it at the time, but she'd copied many of Argentinita's dances, some of which I picked up during these rehearsals.

But when the time came to perform—at La Conga, this time—Anita backed out on me. The night club had billed a sensational Cuban bombshell, Estalita, in letters larger than it had used in billing Anita's. Anita backed out and would not perform. Our agent and my friend, Henry Gine, said I was just as good alone, so I performed without Anita—and was a hit.

I also worked with Teresita Osta, a young woman who'd performed both with Escudero's and Argentinita's companies. But Teresita wasn't really interested in being part of a team. She hoped to become a soloist.

My dancing partners, however, were not nearly as important to me as Meda was. I was gradually becoming completely dependent on her, on her love, on her judgment, and on her guidance.

Whenever I went to Boston or to Chicago, I missed her terribly and wrote her daily—pages and pages, filled with everything that happened to me, everything I thought and felt.

One day, Meda came to me and told me she'd been offered a job as choreographer for a big new show headed for Broadway, which would star Victoria de Cordoba.

"That's wonderful," I said, happy for her.

"Best of all," she told me, "I'll be working with so-and-so, the eminent designer who conceived the show. He's a close friend of mine from years back."

This pleased me, too—at first. Her pleasure was mine. But she went on and on about this old friend. I began to realize they'd been more than friends. I began to get jealous.

I received an offer for a return engagement at the Rumba Casino in Chicago. But before I left, I pleaded with Meda to refuse the choreography assignment she'd taken on. But she wouldn't do it.

I had to go to Chicago anyhow, because of the contract, but I was very upset. As usual, Meda and I exchanged letters. And, in her letters, I began to sense a rather strange indifference—more food for jealousy.

I took a break in my Chicago engagement to come back to New York to see Meda and straighten things out. When my train arrived in Grand Central, at about eight o'clock in the morning, she was there to meet me.

As I saw her, I began to feel the love, assurance, and self-confidence I always felt in her presence. I suggested that we go to the cafe across the street and order some breakfast. Then we began to talk. Or, rather, she began to talk.

"You shouldn't count on me anymore, Gus," she said. "You shouldn't be so dependent on me. You have to get out on your own and do things by yourself."

"But Meda," I said, in these words or words to this effect, "I love you. I need you. How can I do without you? Why must I be independent from you? You are my life."

Her expression grew hard. "Not anymore, Gus, not anymore. It's time for you to stand on your own two legs. It's time for you to be the man you are. I'm not saying I don't love you. I do love you—

much more than you think. But it's time for us to go our separate ways."

"Meda, how can you let this happen?"

"I must, Gus. I don't want you to count on me anymore. You must count on yourself. I'm leaving you right now. You'll never see me again."

I watched her walk away from me, horrified. I understood none of her explanations. I was afraid she'd taken up again with her old friend, the set designer. I felt great pain, then great bitterness.

I went back to Chicago to complete my engagement there, with a cold, angry heart, determined to put Meda out of my mind in any way I could. A way appeared almost immediately, in the shape of a pretty blond girl named Mabel.

Mabel and a girl friend had asked me for an autograph after I performed one night before I'd seen Meda in New York. Now Mabel came back again. Before I knew it, she, her girl friend, the show's pianist, and I were sitting at a hotel bar, having drinks.

I began to joke with Mabel. "What's your apartment like, Mabel? Do you have a nice place?"

"Not bad," she said, grinning. She understood my line of inquiry.

"Would I like it?"

"I suppose so."

"Would you like to show it to me?"

Mabel was a cosmopolitan girl, a buyer for one of Marshal Field's most elegant shops. She always dressed beautifully. But she had a certain provincial exuberance, an inner joy and liveliness I liked very much.

It wasn't long before I found myself in bed with Mabel—and what a marvelous bed partner she was, uninhibited, knowledgeable, and lusty. She knew how to employ every part of her body to heighten the pleasures of love.

Mabel and I began to see each other every night after the show at the Rumba Casino. I enjoyed her company enormously. She wasn't Meda, of course, but she helped me to think of other things, and, in the process, she grew very attached to me.

A few months before, the Japanese had attacked Pearl Harbor. Suddenly, millions of young Americans were joining the Army or waiting around for the draft. From New York, I heard that my old friend Joaquin had entered the service. I was sure my time would come soon, too.

But there I was in Chicago, my engagement at the Rumba Casino about to end, my love with Meda dead, my attentions occupied by Mabel and by the uncertainties that lay ahead. I didn't want to sit around and wait for the draft, but I didn't know what to do.

"I can get you a job here, working for Marshall Field's department store," Mabel told me.

"Is that so?"

"Sure. I know they need presentable young men for the haberdashery department for salesmen."

"Am I presentable?"

She laughed.

So it was set up. That Friday, I went to the employment office and was interviewed. They hired me as a salesman, at thirty-eight dollars a week. I was to start on Monday.

Being a haberdashery salesman didn't have the glamor of dancing, of course. It didn't have the excitement or challenge. But it was a steady job in a time of great uncertainty, and a chance to stay with Mabel, which had its advantages.

I was sleeping late the next morning when the phone rang. It was Mama. She was so excited she could hardly talk.

"Costanzo," she said, when she could collect her wits, "this woman called you. She said she had to speak to you immediately."

"This woman? Who are you talking about?"

"Argentinita. She said her name was Argentinita, the dancer."

"Argentinita!"

"Yes. She told me she'd heard about you through Teresita Osta. Costanzo, she wants you to call her right away, immediately."

"Why? What does she want?"

"I don't know. But she gave me her phone number."

I hung up the phone and called the number Mama had given to me.

"Hello. This is Costanzo Greco. Is this Argentinita?"

"Sí, Señor Greco, sí. ¿Habla usted español?"

In my mind, I blessed Sarita for teaching me Spanish. "Sí, I speak Spanish."

"Well, could you be here tomorrow? I need a new partner, and I want you to audition. If I like you, we'll start rehearsing on Monday."

SEVEN

When I talked to Argentinita, I knew my break had come. And in the face of this opportunity, I could not say, "This is something I have to think over."

I said, "Yes, of course. I'll be there." I didn't think about Mabel, I didn't think about Marshall Field's. I didn't think whether I'd be able to catch a train or a plane. I intended to be in New York the next day even if I had to walk.

So I packed my bags, checked out of my room, and went to the train station. I didn't give a damn when the next train to New York was, I planned to be on it. Sure enough, a train was leaving almost immediately. In those days, trains from Chicago to New York left almost as often as planes do now.

I was so dazed by what had happened that I didn't even call Mabel until Monday, from New York.

"Where are you, you're supposed to be at work."

"I'm not taking the job."

"What?"

"Well, I hope this doesn't upset you too much, but . . ."

And I explained to her what had happened. Fortunately, Mabel was a trouper. She congratulated me and wished me well—and the pleasure in her voice was genuine. I told her I hoped she would come to New York on a buying trip soon, so we could see each other again.

And, a few weeks later, that's exactly what happened. She showed up at my house and talked to my mother, who repeated the conversation to me in her own special way.

Here's the way she told it:

The doorbell rang and Mama opened the door. A pretty blond lady was standing there.

"Where's Greco?" the lady said.

"He's not home. Besides, what do you want my son for?"

"I love your son."

"A lot of women love my son. But what do you *want* with him?"

"I just want to say hello. You know, we met when he was in Chicago, and . . ."

"Hmmn. I no think you good lady for my son."

And Mama sent Mabel away!

Later, we got together several times, on a very pleasant but purely platonic basis. She knew things had changed between us, and she accepted that. This is one of the reasons I'll always have fond memories of her.

Monday morning, I showed up to audition for Argentinita. She told me that her former partner, Federico Rey, had just been drafted, and she needed a replacement for him. Teresita Osta had suggested me.

I had my own worries about the draft, but I kept quiet about them and went through my routines for Argentinita and her sister Pilar Lopez, demonstrating what I'd learned from—among others—Antonio Triana and Anita Sevilla, both of whom had performed with Argentinita.

Argentinita was astonished. "How do you know these dances?" She asked. "Were you born in Spain? Do you have Spanish parents? Have you studied in Spain?"

"No," I admitted. "I learned them from Antonio Triana and Anita Sevilla."

"Anita Sevilla! That bitch, that stealing whore—ever since she left me, she's copied everything I do. How long did you dance with her?"

"A couple of months."

"I don't believe it! What about Triana? How long did you work with him?"

"A week, that's all."

"One week? Incredible! You're lying to me!"

"Why should I? It's the truth. Of course, I've been studying the Spanish dance and performing on and off for eight or nine years now, and . . ."

"What! How old are you?"

"I'm twenty-three years old."

She shook her head, still unwilling to believe what I'd told her. "Go on, show me more."

Now I trotted out all I had learned from Madame Veola, from

Aurora Arriaza, and from my various partners. And I displayed the skills I'd perfected practicing alone in the cellar of my parents' home while everyone else slept.

This had been my habit for some time now. I'd wait until the house was quiet—except, perhaps, for Papa's snoring—then go down to the cellar, close all the doors, put the record player on (with the volume very low), and go to work.

I'd take out the castanets and practice with them for an hour, then put them aside. And then I would practice my footwork for another hour. And then I would practice my turns for still another hour. I muffled my castanets (putting garters around them) and my boot heels, to make as little noise as possible.

By two or three o'clock in the morning, I'd be so exhausted I'd fall asleep on the basement couch and Mama would find me there in the morning when she came downstairs.

When I finished dancing, Argentinita looked at me and smiled. "That was very good, Señor Greco. I've decided to hire you. The job pays seventy-five dollars a week."

"What! Seventy-five dollars a week! The Rumba Casino in Chicago was paying me a hundred dollars a week."

"Well, the job I'm offering you pays seventy-five dollars a week. Take it or leave it. I'm sorry, I can't pay more."

I wasn't there to argue. I'd asked for more because I didn't want to look too anxious. "Of course, I accept your offer," I told her. "I hope you understand that my request was just a matter of business. I'm thrilled that you want me."

"Of course I understand," she said, with a smile of such warmth and grace that I immediately felt great rapport with her. "And if I could pay you more, I would. Right now, we're booked for two weeks. If it goes beyond that, I'll pay you the hundred dollars you're asking."

"*Muy bien*," I said.

I didn't know it then, but Argentinita had good reason not to offer me more than seventy-five dollars. In fact, that was a substantial amount, considering her own somewhat precarious financial situation.

When she and Antonio Triana had split up a couple of years earlier, she'd lost Hurok's sponsorship. Evidently, he thought that Triana was the big drawing card. He wasn't impressed by her new partner, Federico Rey.

Now she was struggling to get bookings, to keep her company alive. Competition from Carmen Amaya and Rosario & Antonio (a team of Spanish dancers who'd learned their art from Carmen Amaya) made things even more difficult.

The problem was a simple one. Big as the United States was, there was room for only so many companies of Spanish dancers. Sure, Spanish dancing was fairly popular here at the time. It was often seen in night clubs, in theaters, and in concert halls.

But it had to compete with all kinds of other touring acts—the big bands, the famous vocalists (both male and female), comedians, magicians, ballroom dance acts, tap dancers, piano players, and everything else you can name.

When I joined Argentinita's company, she had already dropped all but the most important members of her team. In addition to myself, there were Argentinita's sister Pilar; Pablo Miguel (the pianist); and a young, unknown guitarist named Carlos Montoya.

She intended to perform with this group, perhaps augmented by one additional male dancer. Her object was to keep her costs to a minimum, at least until she got a decent number of tour dates.

After we'd been rehearsing a while, Argentinita called me over for a private talk.

"One thing about you bothers me, Costanzo," she said.

"What's that?"

"Your name. How could Costanzo Greco be a Spanish dancer?"

"But I am."

"I know that—and a very fine one, too. But it would be better if you had a Spanish name."

"Fine, if that's what you want. Do you have any suggestions?"

"Well, the last name's okay. After all, El Greco, the painter, is associated with Spain. But Costanzo will never do. How about José?"

"José? José Greco. That sounds good."

I opened with Argentinita in Cincinnati, with the Cincinnati Symphony Orchestra, Eugene Goosens conducting, in the first week of January 1943. A week later, we performed in Rochester, with that city's symphony orchestra, conducted by José Iturbi.

Back in New York, Argentinita, Pilar and her husband, and I spent a great deal of time together. One evening, we went to the Martinique night club to see a sensational young comic named Danny Kaye.

Preceding Danny Kaye on the bill was a team of Spanish dancers.

One of them, a good-looking Mexican boy with a good physique, caught our eye. His name was Manolo Vargas.

As a dancer, Vargas was very much my opposite. I'd usually been described as elegant and suave. He was wild, almost grotesque, his style very animalistic and unrestrained, rather gypsylike.

We needed another male dancer—since, with Argentinita and Pilar, we had two females. So Manolo Vargas was hired. Knowing I might find myself in the Army at any time, I was happy to see him.

We all rehearsed together for a week, during which time it began to look like Vargas wasn't going to make it. He couldn't seem to learn the steps. His style deviated from everyone else's, and he didn't seem able to change it.

Finally, Argentinita let him go.

Vargas came to me in tears. Not only did he not have a job with Argentinita, but also his former partner had left him and stolen what money they'd been able to save.

He inspired my sympathy. Despite his appearance on stage, he was anything but self-confident and masterful. I said, "Well, listen, if you have no place to go, come and live at my house. And while you're there, I'll work with you. Maybe you can get your job back with Argentinita."

Mama—who always gives freely of what she has—took him in and fixed up a room for him. Every day after I came back from rehearsing with the company, I worked with Manolo Vargas.

Finally, after a month of very hard, very intense practice, I felt he'd mastered at least the basics. I felt he could do well enough in the group, if not in duets or solos.

So I went to Argentinita. "Why don't you give Manolo another chance?" I said. "I've been working with him, and I think he can do the job now."

"I don't know. I don't trust him."

"Try him. You'll see."

Finally, she yielded. I brought Manolo to rehearsal the next day, and we all started to rehearse. Before I knew it, without any announcement, he was back in the company.

Then Pilar decided to work up a number with him. She devised a very provocative, very sensual dance—not wild, but seductive. I was very pleased for Manolo.

That afternoon, Mama came to watch the rehearsal, so she saw all of this. On the way home, she warned me about Vargas. "I am a little worried," she said. "Manolo's eccentric style will take the audience's attention from you when both of you are on stage. Be wise and be the showman. Maybe you're a better dancer, but you're too much of a know-it-all."

I had to chuckle. After all, I was Manolo Vargas's instructor. I knew everything he knew—and much more. How could I possibly fear him? I didn't realize how perceptive my mother was.

Then we began to perform together, on the same stage. Suddenly, I found myself in competition with Vargas, at least as the critics saw it. When we performed as guest artists with the Ballet Theater, at least one reviewer found him the far superior dancer.

"José Greco is cool in style, light, controlled, and objective in his approach. At the other end of the scale is a young lad named Manolo Vargas, fleet-footed and fiery, who quite won the hearts of last night's audience. He's definitely somebody to watch," wrote John Martin in the New York *Times*.

He went on to say that I didn't take my dancing seriously enough.

Edwin Denby, writing in the New York *Herald Tribune*, seconded the motion. "The new men partners, Greco and Vargas, were young, handsome and quick. But both seem inexperienced and Greco not serious enough."

It was the first time my work had been criticized by any recognized authorities, and I was really affected by it. I determined to buckle down on stage, to project myself as the artist I knew I was.

In my private relations with Manolo and in rehearsals, there was no duel, no competition. I continued to be his teacher, along with Argentinita. I felt my merit would be recognized eventually and that this critical infatuation with Vargas would pass.

And, indeed, it did.

Reviewing a later performance, a New York *Sun* critic said, "Señor Greco won the audience with the remarkable elasticity and verve of his dancing of the Miller's dance." And, in fact, the curtain opened and closed half a dozen times before the performance could go on. I'd stopped the show.

Edwin Denby, seeing me again, changed his mind. "He is a . . . virtuoso, whose continuity of dancing and exactness of gesture makes his steps very fine indeed."

And John Martin, on second look, said I was "as light and fleet as a cat. This young man can dance!"

Non-New York critics concurred. "Those competent to speak of the dance with any authority feel that José Greco is a superb dancer with perfect rhythmic control," according to a Cincinnati *Post* reviewer.

A writer for the Boston *Herald* said, "He is a young man apparently made of steel springs, handsome and quick, elegant and suave."

In 1943, the New York critics bestowed their ultimate accolade. They voted me the dance newcomer of the year.

This success wasn't just mine, of course. Argentinita was the star of the show, as always. And my triumph was also her triumph.

Not surprisingly, all of this came to the attention of Sol Hurok. He saw the possibilities—Argentinita and her sister Pilar, paired with two young male dancers, one who danced like an animal, the other the epitome of masculine elegance.

Hurok re-engaged Argentinita, this time for a full year of concerts. And she immediately came to me. "Would you accompany us on the tour?" she asked. "I'm willing to pay you $125 a week."

It was no time to argue.

Signing a contract with Hurok had other advantages, too. I remember talking to him about the draft. "They're sure to take me soon," I warned him.

"Well, we wouldn't want that to happen," he said. "That would break up the act. Leave it to me, I'll take care of it."

Soon after, I got the first of several six-month deferments in the mail. And I noticed that among our bookings were a generous sprinkling of military bases and hospitals. Evidently, Hurok had managed to convince the authorities that I was more valuable to the war effort as an entertainer than I would be as a soldier.

At this time in my life, I had no real girlfriends, no deep emotional attachments. If anything, I was under Argentinita's spell. It wasn't that I was in love. It was that I was overflowing with admiration and awe for this great lady almost two decades my senior, who possessed both an incandescent talent and the worldly sophistication to put it to its best use.

Argentinita wasn't beautiful, at least not in the physical sense, like Sophia Loren. But she had personal magnetism that transcended beauty, or the need for it. And she had a look and a smile that could light up any room.

One day, Argentinita asked me to take her to see a new South

American singer who was opening at the Havana Madrid nightclub, a man named Chu Chu Martinez. Chu Chu Martinez, a good-looking fellow with but one arm, had created a sensation with a song called "Besame Mucho." When he sang it, his voice filled with such longing and tenderness that women forgot about his missing arm.

I was astounded when Argentinita asked me to accompany her to the night club to see him, though she intimated there were Spanish dancers on the program she might be interested in seeing. I'd looked at her and danced with her and treated her as the legend she was. Between us, everything was strictly business. It simply had never dawned on me that this person was also a very attractive human being, with human needs, especially the need for companionship.

On the way home, we talked—small talk, I thought.

"Do you have a sweetheart or something?"

"No, not really. Girlfriends, but nothing serious."

We went into her apartment building and up to her door. "I don't have any obligations," I told her, "but I have my moments. Just as I am sure you have yours."

"No, no," she said. "As a matter of fact, I am totally independent."

"That's surprising. I mean, you're a very attractive woman, Argentinita."

She turned toward me with her special look, then a look of such tenderness and yearning that I gave her a very warm and tender kiss, a kiss of respect. If there was any element of sex in it, it was insignificant. But there was anxiety in that kiss, and she sensed it.

The next day, I took her to tea at Rumpelmayer's, near our rehearsal studios. And that night, I took her to dinner. In a certain sense, I began to court her, to establish a close relationship with her. She began to share her ideas and feelings with me.

Suddenly, out of nowhere, Meda called.

EIGHT

I hadn't seen Meda for several months, aside from stopping in to watch the show she'd choreographed (it was not a success, though the fault wasn't hers). I'd pretty much put her out of my mind, though I'd been badly hurt. I felt I'd closed that chapter of my life.

But I hadn't.

Now she told me she wanted very much to see me again—on a personal matter that required a face-to-face meeting.

We got together in a restaurant, as I recall. Meda told me she'd changed her mind, she'd seen the light. She realized that she loved me too much to say good-bye, that she needed me.

"Meda," I said, "it's too late. We can't recapture the enchantment we once had for each other. Too much has happened. We've both suffered too much and cried too much. Besides, I'm so busy with my work, Meda. I have a new direction in life."

"I know," she said, her eyes filled with tears, "but I'm sure I could help you, like before."

"Of course you could help me, I know that. But from now on, you shall help me in my mind, through the beautiful memories of what you showed me, what you taught me."

"But don't you care for me anymore?"

"Care for you? I shall always care for you. I love you dearly. And you will always occupy a special place in my thoughts and in my heart."

This is true, even now. I think of Meda as an angel.

She cried at my words, and I tried my best to comfort her.

"Don't be hurt, Meda. Remember what we had together. Remember what you taught me. You made me what I am now. You taught me that I must be objective, that I must see life as it really is, not as I might hope it was."

"I know."

"And I know it's also true that we cannot go back to the way things were before. I hope we always remain friends, but it can no longer be more than that."

She looked and nodded and understood.

"Now I have to say good-bye, Meda. I must leave you. I have a rehearsal appointment with Argentinita in twenty minutes."

I walked Meda to the subway and said good-bye to her there. Then I turned from her and started to walk away.

Suddenly, I heard a thumping noise and the sound of women screaming. Meda had fainted and fallen all the way down the subway steps. I looked into the entrance and saw her prostrate form lying on the bottom landing.

I vaulted down the stairs, pushed through the crowd that had gathered around her, and picked her up in my arms. She moaned, then opened her eyes. She wasn't really hurt—at least physically—because she'd fainted before she'd fallen.

I forgot about my rehearsal and rode with her on the subway all the way back to Brooklyn. Our conversation was mainly about the past—about the night of Joe Atlas's party, about Madame Veola, about seeing Carmen Amaya.

During the ride, somehow, we did recapture the feelings we'd had for each other—but not in such a way as to renew them. Instead, Meda began to realize her purpose in my life, the marvelously generous thing she'd done for me, making me what I was. And she realized that I'd been right, that she could no longer be to me what she once had been.

When we said good-bye, at her stop, there was tranquillity and affection between us. We each knew we'd never forget the other. And Meda knew I'd always think of her with the greatest admiration and fondness.

Once more, I closed that chapter of my life—this time without the bitterness, with a love that, in a way, still endures.

In the months that followed, Argentinita and I grew steadily closer, despite the differences in our ages and stations in life. We increasingly turned to each other for companionship, for someone with whom to share life's joys and troubles.

Again, I found myself with a woman who knew far more about my art and about life than I did. Again, I found myself learning and growing because of what a woman could teach me and show me.

Argentinita told me about her past, in detail. She'd been born in Argentina, but her parents were pure Castilians. She was raised in Spain. Her father had loved flamenco and had taken her, when she was just a child, to all of the cafes where flamenco was played, sung, or danced.

These experiences, which began almost as soon as she was able to walk, were the source of her great artistry. And in a very real way, they became one of the bases of my art, too, since she transmitted them to me with breathtaking vividness.

We talked for hours without end about Argentinita's Spain, about the origins of the Spanish dance, about Spain's cultural heritage. We also talked about her great friends in Spain. She was part of a circle not unlike that Gertrude Stein had gathered about herself in Paris a couple of decades earlier, a circle that included Manuel de Falla, Ortega y Gasset, Garcia Lorca, Edgar Neville, Pastora Imperial, Gregorio Maranon, Domingo Ortega, José Maria Penon, and other great people.

Through Argentinita, I came to know the true meaning of the Spanish dance, the history and culture of Spain itself, and the spirit that kept it bright. I came to know so much of what there was to know about Spain's most outstanding musicians, dancers, poets, bullfighters, patriots, and politicians that I felt as if I *were* Spanish— all this though I'd never set foot on Spanish soil.

There was a certain penalty attached to this relationship, however. Inevitably, I began to draw resentment from some of the other members of the company, particularly Argentinita's sister Pilar Lopez, and Argentinita's maid, a woman named Teresa.

Pilar Lopez saw me as an upstart and an opportunist. She'd had no part in discovering me, so she had no stake in me. As far as she was concerned, I was untried, unproven, and easily replaced. No amount of critical acclaim or adulation from our audiences could ever change that.

Argentinita's maid seemed to dislike me more and more the closer I got to the lady she served. To this day, I do not understand why. At least at first, I was never anything less than polite to Teresa. It may be that she was jealous, that she harbored her own passion for Argentinita.

I got along well enough with the other members of the company. In Manolo Vargas's case, I continued to be the teacher. But in at least one instance, involving Carlos Montoya, I was the student.

In those days, Montoya was a young man, about my age, a little rough, a little wild, a friendly fellow but unpolished. Montoya was really the only fellow in the company with whom I could have a few laughs.

He was a gypsy from Madrid, a strange combination of sophistication and primitivism. He sometimes warned me to be careful with Argentinita and Pilar because they were powerful women who could "really do the voodoo on you," if they wanted.

Mostly, though, we talked of Spanish music and Spanish dance. "I want to dance better," I told him. "I want to dance as well as anyone has ever danced. I want to learn everything there is to learn about the Spanish dance."

"Oh," he said, "well, if that's the case, I can teach you. I can teach you an allegrias."

An allegrias was a typical flamenco dance—exactly the sort of thing I wanted to learn. "You know how to do an allegrias?" I asked. "Show me."

He did a few steps. And I said to myself, my God, this man really knows how to dance. But maybe that wasn't so surprising. All gypsies —whether they're singers or guitarists or even janitors—seem to know how to dance, at least a little. "Okay," I said, "teach me."

"Fine. That will be fifteen dollars a class."

A member of my own company asking money to teach me a dance? I could hardly believe it. When I was teaching Manolo, that idea had never occurred to me. But this, too, was typical of a gypsy. "That's too much money," I said. "I'll pay you fifty dollars if you teach me the whole routine."

We made a deal. For the next few weeks, Montoya taught me what he knew—a few small things, it turned out, but quite effective in their way.

Later, I told Argentinita of our transaction.

"What? He charged you money? I can't believe it!"

"It's true."

She laughed. "That gypsy! Well, at least he was honest and straightforward about it."

Over the years, Montoya changed. He became a man. More than that, he became a gentleman. Some of this, no doubt, was due to the very positive influence of his wife, Sally, who played a role in his life not unlike that Meda—and Argentinita—played in mine.

In this period—the early 1940s—Argentinita was very friendly with the Marquis de Cuevas, a Chilean aristocrat who lived in New York and who'd married a Rockefeller.

The Marquis de Cuevas was a devoted patron of the arts. He was especially taken with the Spanish dance, and he personally knew all of the great artists in that field of whom I have already spoken.

He was also interested in the opera, and through acquaintances in that field had come to know my sister Norina. Her eminence as a singer was increasing rapidly. After the 1942 Met season closed, she was invited to tour South America with Grace Moore, Lawrence Tibbett, Martinelli, and several other big stars.

The Marquis de Cuevas was famous for, among other things, his lavish parties. He often invited various artists to his home, to eat, drink—and perform. Before I'd joined the company, he'd given a party for Argentinita, Carmen Amaya, and Rosario & Antonio. Reportedly, that one almost turned into a slugfest.

As it happened, there was bad blood between Carmen Amaya and the dance team Rosario & Antonio. She'd been their boss and had taught them much of what they knew. When they left her, they "borrowed" her choreographies and routines and became a big success, thereby earning her eternal enmity.

Anyhow, when they started to perform a dance at one of the Marquis de Cuevas's parties, Carmen Amaya got up and said, "You're not going to do that dance, because it's my dance and I have to do it." Before the party was over, they nearly came to blows —or so I heard. I wasn't there.

I was invited to a later party, however, along with Argentinita and her company, Andres Segovia, my sister, and other great personalities. Segovia was already a star—I'd seen his face on those posters at Detroit's Masonic Temple when I was nothing but a dishwasher.

We all danced for the Marquis—Argentinita and Pilar, Manolo and I. And he was so excited about what he saw that he decided to include Argentinita's company in a concert he was sponsoring at the Museum of Modern Art (which, itself, had been built largely through the donations of the Rockefeller family).

It was an incredible event, and again Vargas stole the show. Yet the entire performance was so sensational that Hurok, who was in attendance, immediately began to renegotiate with Argentinita, and Salvador Dali offered to do the decors for one of our ballets.

All of this inspired such enthusiasm that the Marquis decided to sponsor a Spanish festival at the Metropolitan Opera House the following May.

And at that festival, Dali did the sets, José Iturbi conducted the orchestra, and Argentinita enlarged the company, engaging many of the Spanish dancers and soloists then in New York. That night was such a success that Hurok, entirely apart from the regular concerts he arranged for Argentinita and her ensemble, gave her a contract to be guest artist with the Ballet Theater.

At this time, I recaptured my younger years with Muriel Bentley, Nora Kaye, and Jerome Robbins, who had just created his sensational ballet *Fancy Free*.

Now I was in the midst of the great world of dance and music, in contact with people such as Leonard Bernstein, Antony Tudor, Agnes De Mille, Lucia Chase, Oliver Smith, André Eglevsky, Igor Youskevitch, and so many other great stars of the dance. I was in heaven.

Even amid this remarkable panoply of talent, Argentinita and her company—myself included—were standouts. And after the show, the Marquis de Cuevas made a special point of congratulating me and Manolo Vargas.

In fact, the Marquis' attentions went beyond congratulations. Knowing we were young dancers, not earning a fortune, he offered to put us up at his large, luxurious townhouse until we could afford truly suitable quarters of our own. In my innocence, I thought this was another example of his philanthropy.

There seemed no reason not to accept. His house was far more convenient to rehearsals than my own (my family now lived in the Bronx). Besides, it would give me the opportunity to meet many interesting and important poeple.

Manolo Vargas and I accepted his offer and moved in. We soon found we weren't the only ones. A number of other young men lived with the Marquis: a blond fellow, a thin fellow, a black fellow, a dark-haired fellow, etc.

I found this all very strange. I also found it strange when the Marquis presented me with a bankbook in which a $1,000 deposit had been made in my name. This was my very first bank account. I shrugged my shoulders, though, and promptly took $850 and bought

57

myself a $1,000 savings bond—in case he wanted to be paid back—and used the other $150 to meet my needs.

One night, the Marquis visited my room. He told me how handsome I was, how virile I looked when I danced, how lithe my body was—that sort of thing. He wanted me very badly.

I didn't want to offend the man—after all, he was my benefactor. But this sort of activity just wasn't my style. I never went in that direction. I always went in the other direction, perhaps too much so.

"I'm not cut from that particular bolt of cloth," I told him. "I don't have anything against it, you understand"—which was true enough—"but it just isn't for me"—which was also true.

The Marquis entreated me. He pleaded with me. He cajoled and begged and offered further, more magnificent benevolences. He spoke about creating a great ballet company for Argentinita, in which I would play a major role.

I managed to put him off. In fact, I managed to establish a platonic relationship with him, or so I thought. We did have other things to talk about, since his interest in the art, in dance, was quite genuine.

Then one day Argentinita found out where I was staying.

"You're like all the rest of the sons-of-bitches," she told me. "And I thought you were a man, with balls."

"Wait a minute," I said, "don't accuse me like this. It's not what you think. Besides, you introduced me to him. I thought I was doing you a favor by being nice to him. He has all kinds of plans for you."

"There's nothing he can do for me," Argentinita said, contemptuously. "I don't care what he says. Anyhow, I thought you were a man, not a mouse."

"I'm only staying there to be closer to town, to rehearse, or so I can take you out to dinner more conveniently."

"You expect me to believe that? Everyone knows about the Marquis de Cuevas. If you stay there, it can mean only one thing."

Pretty soon, she had me feeling like an idiot. And she had me convinced I'd better get out of that townhouse if I wanted to save my reputation. More than that, by her actions she'd also convinced me that she cared for me even more than she'd let on.

The next morning, I packed my bag and started for the door of the townhouse. The Marquis suddenly appeared in front of me, between me and the front door.

"José, where are you going?"

"I'm leaving, Jorge. Thanks for everything, but I have to go now."

"But why? Haven't I been good to you?"

"Very good, Jorge. There's no denying it. But I'm going back to my parents' house."

"Someone has poisoned your mind against me. Someone is behind this, I'm sure of it."

"There's no one behind it. I'm behind it, only me."

"Why don't you stay, then?"

"I can't stay. What am I doing here? My mother says I have a beautiful home, and why am I not home? And you know my mother, you know my sister—they want me home."

He moved to block the doorway completely. "I don't care what they say. You belong to me. I'm going to do all kinds of wonderful things for you. I'm going to . . ."

"Listen, Jorge, let's cut out the crap. I'm leaving, and that's that."

"No you're not." He pushed me away from the door. I pushed back. He shoved me again. I can't believe he felt so strongly about me. It must have been a matter of pride. Maybe he'd bet someone that he'd have Greco, even if it took months.

I finally bulled my way past him and out the front door and into the fresh air. And that was the end of my relationship with the Marquis de Cuevas.

Now I headed for Argentinita. I had to know exactly how deeply she felt about me.

NINE

After depositing my bag at the family residence in the Bronx, I went directly to Argentinita's place.

"All right," I told her. "I know where I live. I live at 238th Street and White Plains Road—and not at the Marquis de Cuevas's townhouse."

"Well, well, I'm glad to hear it."

"You know," I said, "we'll be performing in such-and-such a place tomorrrow night—not far from here."

"Of course I know. Why do you mention it?"

"Well, I'm going to take a hotel room near the theater. Can I reserve a room there for you? I'd like you to stay there, rather than go back to your apartment in New York. I'd like to talk to you."

It was a very bold leap for me, this suggestion of intimacy. But I felt if Argentinita could scold me about the Marquis de Cuevas on such a personal basis, I could talk to her on the same level.

I wanted to meet with her and talk with her on my ground, not on her ground. And I didn't want to risk interruption by her maid or her sister or another member of the company. I wanted the meeting to be just between us.

Argentinita looked at me for a long time. I began to think I had made a mistake. She was, after all, a woman of considerable magnitude. She was also older and more worldly than I. What could I be to her?

"All right," she said, finally, "reserve a room for me."

So began an intimate relationship, a romance, that lasted until Argentinita's death. It was a covert romance, a hidden relationship, however. We both wanted it that way, because of the differences in our ages and positions, because of her worldwide eminence. I speak of it here for the very first time.

Looking back, I feel great pride in what Argentinita and I were to one another. Our relationship was not predicated upon our professional lives or what we did on stage. It was totally personal, filled with warmth and affection of the noblest sort. It was never vulgar, never used against anyone else.

Ever since I'd joined Argentinita's company, Pilar Lopez and others had called me an opportunist. But here is the proof that I was not. My relationship with Argentinita, though unknown to anyone else, was so strong and so intense that I could easily have asked her for anything.

If I wanted to, I could have gotten rid of Manolo Vargas, for instance, and made myself the one and only male dancer in the company—the star. I even could have gotten rid of Pilar Lopez herself, since the relationship between the sisters was often troubled. But I did no such thing.

Instead, I partook of an extraordinary personal fulfillment, nurtured by Argentinita's intelligence, depth of feeling, and womanliness. True, we had to steal our moments of love and of companionship. But this was enough for me. I neither sought nor desired another serious love interest.

Professionally, my stature grew—and not always with Argentinita's immediate approval. I began to make suggestions on what dances we should perform, in what order, and with what settings. Sometimes, Argentinita—often along with Pilar—violently disagreed with my ideas.

There was one occasion when I had an idea for choreographing an entire dance. I was sure I could improve upon the way the company was doing it. At first, Argentinita and Pilar were sure I was wrong. They felt that audiences would hate my conception.

But I argued and cajoled and finally convinced them to let me at least try it, in front of one audience. It was the hit of our performance. Not only did the audience go wild, the critics also strongly approved.

To apologize—and to thank me—Argentinita had a ring made for me in San Francisco, and she gave it to me. No one knew it, of course, but that ring was more than a token of appreciation. It also honored the feeling Argentinita and I had for each other.

Of course, the theater and the dance being what they are, there were other women in my life from time to time—passing encounters of no lasting significance. There was one woman, however, whom I shall always remember, a woman named Phoebe.

I first met Phoebe in 1943, when I was performing with Argentinita and her company in California. We'd toured the entire country under Hurok's sponsorship, playing to large, enthusiastic audiences, winning critical plaudits, winding up on the West Coast.

There, Jeannette Cozzone, an old friend of mine from the days of Madame Veola, spotted my name in a newspaper ad. She guessed that José Greco was none other than the Costanzo Greco she'd known a few years earlier.

At any rate, she invited me to stay at her house—she'd married an aeronautical engineer—for the time I'd be in California, and I accepted. We spent many hours reliving the old days.

After a while, she mentioned that she had a friend she was sure would like me and vice versa. "Why don't I call her up and introduce you over the phone and you can invite her to dinner."

Well, this is what happened. After speaking a few minutes to her friend Phoebe, Jeannette handed me the phone. "Hello," I said, "my name is José Greco."

She said, "Well, my name is Phoebe So-and-so."

"That's a beautiful name."

"Thank you," she said. "And I have to tell you that you have the sexiest telephone voice I've ever heard. I've got to meet you."

She joined us at Jeannette's house for dinner that evening.

Physically, Phoebe was not unlike Susan Hayward, the movie actress—not quite as pretty, perhaps, but just as elegant, and even more buxom. Phoebe was from the Southwest—Oklahoma or Texas —and, temperamentally, a joyous, free-spirited, happy-go-lucky woman.

In her professional life, Phoebe was a manager and agent. She managed the career of a Broadway dancer who'd made quite a name for herself, and she was the agent of a well-known actor.

At any rate, I found her beauty, her charm, her wonderful southwestern drawl captivating. Over dinner that night, we teased each other constantly, our conversation full of sexual innuendos, the witty kind rather than the crude variety.

After a couple of days, as these things go, we found ourselves in her apartment. I think I told her that I wanted to practice my sexy voice on her, or some such nonsense. I didn't anticipate what actually happened.

"José," she said, "tonight, I'm going to make you an Indian chief. Just lie down on the bed. You don't have to move a muscle."

This sounded promising. I did what I'd been told. "Okay, go to work."

Phoebe proceeded to strip me, then herself. Then she made love to me in the most incredible manner I had ever—or have ever—experienced. She did things that I'd never even heard of—many things.

I know Xaveria Hollander has written books about her sexual knowledge, but, believe me, Phoebe could have written a book that would have shamed her or any other sexual expert.

With Phoebe, sex was truly an art. And she was its great master. She made me feel like an ignoramus. She made me feel wonderful beyond belief. She made me feel like an Indian chief, or a king.

But she didn't let me lift a finger. She was the producer, director, and star of the show. It was such a wonderful show that I didn't care. It was the ultimate love experience. Furthermore, it was suffused with her warm sense of humor and with the generosity of her spirit.

Phoebe gave of herself totally, without restraint. She wanted me to experience every aspect of her, to have sex with me with her whole being. And, with her all-encompassing knowledge and prodigious skill, she succeeded.

Once more, I found myself the student of a magnificent woman. Meda was an angel, Argentinita, incomparable. Phoebe, however, was a sex goddess—and, on those nights we spent together, my own personal sex goddess.

I believe that Phoebe even fell in love with me. But this relationship was not destined to be a romance, at least not from my side. Our approaches were too different.

Phoebe, in bestowing her wondrous joys, was interested only in giving. She wasn't comfortable with or interested in receiving. I felt that love—or even sex, for that matter—involved a give-and-take.

In 1944, when our company returned to California, I saw Phoebe again. It was no less glorious than before, but no more likely to lead to anything permanent.

During this period, I met one other woman worth mentioning, if only because of the enormously important role she was to play in my life: Lucille Peters.

When I first came across her, Lucille Peters was dancing at the studio of La Meri, in New York. La Meri was a famous ethnic dancer, whose range even included dances of the Middle East.

I went to her studio with Argentinita, to see some of La Meri's students. One of them was a pretty, dark-haired young girl from West Virginia, a girl of Lebanese background who'd been raised mainly in Brooklyn—Lucille Peters.

She was a charming little creature, with a wide smile and shining eyes. She was also a rather good dancer. We talked briefly, as I recall, and I put her name away in my memory, knowing that I'd want to talk to her again one day.

But my main attentions, both personally and professionally, were focused on Argentinita. We did our best to hide the romance between us, and I think we succeeded. Nevertheless, it was obvious to Pilar and to Teresa (Argentinita's maid) that we were building an enduring friendship.

By this time, Hurok had made us a permanent part of his Ballet Theater touring group. I was earning between $250 and $300 a week, and I was acting almost as a company manager, attending to the lights, the sets, and the costumes (in addition to my role as a performing artist).

But so far as Pilar and Teresa were concerned, Argentinita was treating me with too much regard. Argentinita asked for my opinion in reference to a dance, in reference to a color, in reference to a costume, and she listened to me when I gave it. She paid less and less attention to Pilar's opinions.

When Pilar criticized me behind my back, Manolo supported her. Possibly he would have acted differently if I'd charged him when I taught him, as Carlos Montoya had charged me. As it was, he probably resented me, as many students resent the teacher who lifts them out of ignorance, especially if his lessons are free.

As a result, there came to be open animosity between Pilar and myself. And because of this state of affairs, Teresa thought that she, too, had the license to snarl insolently at me whenever the mood struck her (except when Argentinita was listening). Teresa saw no difference in our stations.

The trouble between Argentinita's maid and I came to a head in the fall of 1944, in St. Louis. We were packing up in the theater, after our last performance of that engagement, when the conflict took on a new dimension.

I don't remember now what Teresa had done wrong—or even if she thought I'd done something wrong—but it began with an argument about some trivial matter, something of no importance. We

1. Montorio Nei Frentani, the village of my birth.

2. Norina, Mama, and myself, looking like I'm about to start crying. This picture was taken in 1923.

3. Montorio, 1926. I'm the chubby-faced little boy sitting at the extreme left. A fair portion of the rest are aunts, uncles, and cousins. Standing near the right edge is the priest who taught us.

4. My passport photo. I'm wearing the white flannel suit my father sent me.

5. Norina and I in Brooklyn, in a photo taken in August 1928. I had no idea then what role the photographer would play in my life.

6. Myself, Norina, Mama, and Papa, taken in Brooklyn in August 1928. We wore our very best.

7. This yellowed, blurry photograph is the only picture I have of myself at Madame Veola's studio. It was taken, I believe, in 1933. I wasn't quite fifteen.

8. Madame Helene Veola, my first dancing teacher, in a picture taken some thirty years before I met her.

9. Myself (top right, grinning and waving) with my friends at the art school, in a photo taken in the early 1930s.

10. Myself and my first wife, Sarita, taken in about 1936 (PHOTO CREDIT: BRUNO OF HOLLYWOOD).

11. Myself and my second partner, Gloria Belmonte, in the late 1930s (PHOTO CREDIT: BRUNO OF HOLLYWOOD).

12. Myself and Teresa McCall, at a Westchester country club in September 1940.

13. Teresa McCall, myself, and Meda, looking pensive and beautiful as usual.

ended up screaming and yelling at each other, her vile language putting my knowledge of Spanish swear words to its ultimate test.

What I couldn't understand was why her feelings were so violent, so out of proportion to the argument of the moment. It was as if I'd grievously injured her somehow, or ridiculed her for all the world to see. But that was Teresa's style. I swallowed my anger and forgot the episode.

That night, we boarded the train for Chicago. We were scheduled to perform there the next afternoon. Teresa boarded the train ahead of me, sniping and snarling all the way. I told her to cut the nonsense and get on the train.

As I stepped onto the landing, she turned. "Here," she barked, "this is for what you said to me in the theater this afternoon." Then she reared back and smashed me in the nose with all the strength she possessed.

I fell down, out of the train, landing on the station platform, stunned, at Argentinita's feet. I got up with murder in my eye. I didn't care who Teresa was, whether or not she was a woman. I felt like I wanted to kill her. Argentinita stopped me with a few soft words.

I got onto the train and went to my compartment, feeling humiliated, ashamed, and hurt. What the hell is going on? I asked myself. Why should this happen?

My mind was buzzing. I thought, maybe I deserve this. Maybe I'm a son-of-a-bitch that no one likes. Maybe I don't belong with Argentinita and the company at all.

A few minutes later, Argentinita arrived, along with the porter, who was carrying a bucket of ice. She put it on my nose tenderly and ministered to me.

"Why should this happen, Encarna?" (Argentinita's given name was Encarnación.)

"Please, José. Rest, be calm."

"I mean, what is wrong with that woman? What is wrong with Pilar and Manolo? Why is everyone against me?"

She looked at me quietly for a moment, as though reluctant to say what was on her mind. But she did. "It's because I love you, José. And they know it."

"Then why don't you tell everyone? Why don't you tell the world?"

"I can't, José. You know that. You know how it would look."

65

She was right.

I didn't sleep during the trip to Chicago. My mind was aboil with the humiliation I'd suffered at Teresa's hands.

The next afternoon, at Orchestra Hall in Chicago, I was totally miserable. My nose had turned purple and had swollen to enormous size. I could hardly breathe. I could hardly talk.

Make-up covers many sins, however. That day, it allowed me to perform without anyone in the audience being aware of my distress, that and my determination not to disappoint Argentinita.

After the show, I headed for my dressing room, sweating, panting for breath, exhausted. Suddenly, there was Teresa, between me and my dressing room door.

She looked at me with total loathing. "You son-of-a-bitch," she began.

The fury welled up in me instantly. I took a roundhouse swing at her and connected, bashing her in the nose, sending her flying all the way across the stage (behind the curtain, of course).

She landed in a heap, her nose broken and bleeding.

This seemed to me exactly as it should be. I made no move to help her. Instead, I went into my dressing room and changed. Later, I heard that she'd called the police and reported the whole thing.

When we got back to New York, I was summoned to the offices of Sol Hurok himself.

"Hey, Greco. How are you?" He greeted me with a smile and a handshake.

"I'm fine," I said. "What can I do for you?"

"I understand you stabbed a woman in Chicago," he said.

I laughed. "Come on, Pop." (Everyone called Hurok Pop.) "I may be Italian, but I'm not that violent. I'm not the Mafioso type. I just don't have any violence in me. I can't even look at a knife. I can't stand the sight of blood."

"Maybe so, but from what I hear, the Chicago police have a warrant out for your arrest, charging that you stabbed a woman named Teresa Martinez. And she says she has witnesses."

"What!? That's ridiculous! She hit me in the nose and I hit her back. Believe me, she deserved it. But that's all there was to it."

"Maybe so, maybe so. That's not the point, however."

"What is the point, then?" I had a feeling I knew what was coming.

"I can't have this kind of thing happening to my performers,"

Hurok said. "It doesn't look right. Nothing personal, you understand, but I think you'd better find other work."

"So that's what you think. What does Argentinita think?"

Hurok sighed. "She just left. She's on your side, José. More so than I expected, to tell you the truth. She pointed out that she'd signed a contract with you that ran through the end of the season."

"That's true," I said.

"I pointed out that every contract carries a clause that says it's void if the signer commits any misdeed or public offense."

"But I did nothing of the sort."

"That's what Argentinita said. If you can prove that, or if you can get the Chicago police to drop their warrant, I'll honor your contract. But I'm afraid it has to be the last one between us, José. Personally, I like you—you know that. And you're an outstanding dancer. But Hurok can't have anything to do with the police."

"Yes, of course. I understand." I was furious—but what could I do?

I went to Argentinita, who was at least as upset as I. "He gave me no choice, José."

"I know, believe me, I know."

"Now we have to figure out how to get the Chicago police off your back."

Argentinita ended up calling the most influential man she could think of· the Marquis de Cuevas, of all people. She explained what had happened. And, to his credit, he saw to it that the warrant was dropped.

But now Argentinita and I both had a problem. She'd need a new partner for the 1945–46 season. As for me, I needed a new job. Our relationship was undamaged by all of this. We decided to help each other as best we could.

We talked about it at length. She'd help me put together a company of my own. I'd help her audition new partners. We'd go our separate ways professionally, though not personally.

There were only two difficulties. The first was Pilar Lopez, who was demanding equal billing with her sister and threatening to quit if she didn't get what she wanted. The second was Argentinita's health. She had a persistent fever. It would come, get better, then return, worse than before.

TEN

This sickness of Argentinita's had been coming and going ever since the beginning of the 1944–45 season. At first, it didn't bother me very much. What does a fever mean? Usually, not much.

But in the spring of 1945, I began to worry. There'd been a distinct change in Argentinita's eye color. Before, she'd had sparkling eyes—gleaming brown irises surrounded by the clearest possible white. Now her eyes seemed lackluster. Sometimes I caught a tinge of yellow, possibly even a hint of red.

Other things worried me more, however: I had to make plans for the next season. I remembered Lucille Peters. With her, I thought, I might have the core of a company. I contacted her, and she enthusiastically agreed to join me.

Then, with Argentinita's help, I found a guitarist and a pianist, both essential to any Spanish dance company. She also helped with costumes, music, and routines, at least when she was feeling well enough.

While I continued to perform with Argentinita's company, knowing I'd be out of a job when the summer began, I also started calling hotels and resorts throughout New England. Before long, I'd arranged a modest schedule for Lucille and myself, to begin when my contract with Argentinita ran out.

In my off hours, I rehearsed with Lucille Peters, in a studio I'd rented in the *Hobo News* building. The more I saw of this girl, the more I liked her. She was quick, petite, and she had an endearing innocence. It was hard not to like her, to be attracted to her. We began to see each other even when we weren't rehearsing.

She did present one problem, however: Lucille Peters was an even more ridiculous name for a Spanish dancer than Costanzo Greco had been. I decided to rename her, as Argentinita had renamed me.

For her first name, I chose Nila (knee-la), taking it from the Nile River, in Egypt, in honor of Lucille's Arabic background. For her new last name, I chose the Spanish word Amparo, which means protectress. And so Lucille Peters became Nila Amparo.

As spring approached, the end of my professional association with Argentinita also drew near. But there were still some glorious moments ahead. On April 11, we were to perform at the Metropolitan Opera House for a Spanish war benefit, repeating the festival of two years before, in front of sets designed by Salvador Dali, to the accompaniment of the New York Philharmonic, as conducted by José Iturbi.

I remember that night vividly, not so much because it was a triumph in every way—which it surely was—but because an incident occurred then that illustrates just how mean and petty dancers, especially Spanish dancers, can be to each other.

As Manolo Vargas and I were heading up the stairs to our dressing rooms, we met Antonio—of Rosario & Antonio—descending. Evidently, he'd just come from Argentinita's dressing room, after having wished her luck on this auspicious occasion.

Antonio, a cocky little man, passed by us on the outside of the stairs, closer to Vargas than to me. And as he passed by, he made some kind of remark to Vargas, I couldn't hear what. From his expression and his tone of voice, I knew he wasn't wishing us luck.

"What did he say, Manolo?"

Vargas shrugged. "He gave us the *alternativa*."

I knew enough about bullfighting, through my conversations with Argentinita, to understand what that meant. The *alternativa* is what the professional bullfighter says to the novice on the day the novice is to take the field. In bullfighting, it is frequently an emotional moment, rather like graduation.

In this situation, however, it was nothing of the sort. It was an insult, nothing less. Manolo and I were not novices. I, especially, was a professional dancer of considerable experience and repute. I'd danced with symphony orchestras all over the country. I'd danced in Carnegie Hall. Antonio had danced in none of those places. He was a popular night club performer, nothing more.

I'm not saying which one of us was the better dancer. Who knows? But I am saying that my stature was equal to his. That night, when he gave us the *alternativa*, he proved that he was a small man in more ways than one. Instead of wishing us luck, he allowed his bitterness and jealousy to show through clearly.

It turned out that we didn't need his best wishes. The performance was a remarkable success. We received nothing more than a dozen curtain calls, and the next morning's papers were full of praise for every member of the company.

Sometime later, his night club business exhausted, Antonio (with Rosario, his partner) had his manager get him a concert booking in New York. I wasn't in town that evening—I was in Philadelphia or Washington, I forget which.

At any rate, I heard about his opening. So I sent him a telegram:

> "Dear Antonio, Tonight, I give you the *alternativa*.
> José Greco."

I suppose you might say I was responding to Antonio's pettiness with some of my own. But I felt entitled.

In May 1945, I performed with Argentinita for the last time. It was a sad occasion for both of us. Afterward, we talked about the future. Argentinita wasn't sure what she was going to do next—continue touring, retire, or perform only occasionally. She'd come to a crossroads in her life. She was ready to break off with her sister.

One of Argentinita's ideas was to return to Spain and do a farewell tour, not with her company, but just with me. This idea excited her more than any other. "Would you do it, José?"

"Of course, Encarna."

In June, Nila and I began our own little tour, in Vermont and New Hampshire. By this time, I was thoroughly taken with her childlike candor, her simple, sweet attitude toward life, her kindness, her desire to learn. And she was smitten with me. I was a man of the world by this time—I was all of twenty-six.

Inevitably, we began to fall in love—not with the passion that had marked my relationship with Meda or even with Argentinita, but with a gentle tenderness, a deep affection. It was a beautiful love.

With Meda and Argentinita, I'd been constantly challenged to prove myself, to grow, to be more than I had been. Both women were quite capable of taking care of themselves without my help. With Nila, there was no challenge. I was the teacher. She depended on me, possibly to too great an extent.

In that period, I felt that I must take care of Nila, that she needed me, that I must support her. Only later did I discover that she could be as tough and independent as any woman I'd ever known.

Ironically, at about the same time I was going through my career changes, my sister's career was also in trouble. By the time she'd returned to America from South America, Italy had joined Germany in World War II.

Jealous competitors had started a whispering campaign that Norina was pro-Italian and pro-Fascist. It was nonsense, but it was the sort of nonsense there's no way to stop.

Norina is a proud woman. She refused to humble herself, to deny what was being said about her, to beg for anything. When the director of the Metropolitan Opera told her he wouldn't be needing her anymore, she made no attempt to clear the air.

Instead, she said that if the Met didn't need her, she didn't need the Met. She told the director that the Met was decadent, immoral, filled with jealousies and prejudices. That was the end of her career at the Met. After that, she began touring—as a guest performer in various opera companies throughout the United States.

Just after Nila and I began our own tour in New England, Argentinita called me to say she was going into the hospital for some tests, at her doctor's request.

"When I get out," she said, "I'll go to Spain and set up our tour."

"Fine, Encarna. Just let me know when you want me to come. I'll join you in Spain and rehearse with you and tour with you as long as you want. Then we'll talk about the future."

Argentinita was in and out of the hospital all summer long. Early in September, she called me in New Hampshire. She'd had an operation, and the doctors had found a malignancy.

"Please come back José. I want to see you before I die."

"Die? You must be joking. What are you talking about, dying?"

"It's true, José, I know it is. If you want to see me again, you'll have to hurry back to New York."

I remember driving back in the dead of night, still half dressed in my costume. I went directly to the hospital. At the desk, they told me that Argentinita was in critical condition, that she couldn't have visitors.

The hell with that, I told myself. I climbed some back stairs and found her room. She was lying there in bed, deathly pale, but somehow very beautiful.

"Thank God you've come, José," she said. "I only have a few days to live."

"Please, Encarna, don't say that. You have so many things to live for. You promised to introduce me to all of your wonderful friends in Spain. You promised to show me your beautiful house on Majorca. You promised to take me with you on tour. Now you tell me that you're going to die? You can't die. Not now, not yet."

"I'm sorry, José, but I am going to die. Come and give me a kiss on the cheek."

I bent down to her bed and kissed her.

At that instant, a nurse appeared at the door, horrified. "What are you doing in here? Who let you in? You get out of here or I'll call the doctor. I'll call the orderly and have you thrown out."

I smiled at Argentinita, who smiled back almost imperceptibly. Then I left. I drove back to New Hampshire, where I had to perform that night with Nila.

A week or ten days later, Argentinita's brother-in-law—Pilar's husband—called me. I was at another hotel in New England. "Argentinita has fallen into a coma," he told me. "She may not last the day." That was September 24, 1945.

Nila and I drove back to New York, but we were too late. Argentinita died before we arrived at the hospital.

Time stopped for me that day. It was the first time in my life that anyone I'd really cared about had died. And I had really cared about Argentinita. She was part of me. She remains part of me to this day.

We rushed to the hospital, as people often do in these circumstances, though there wasn't a thing we could do except mourn. And mourn we did—Pilar and her brother, even Teresa, the maid (who'd long since been fired).

The strangest thing happened then: Everyone's attitude toward me did a complete turnabout. Envy and distrust turned into admiration, even adoration.

"You were the only one who helped, José."

"You were the only one who really knew her."

"Only you gave her real comfort, José."

Coming from Pilar—even from Teresa—this was almost too much to bear.

"Forgive me, José, give me an embrace," Pilar said.

I couldn't contain my bitterness. "Why should I embrace you? Because your sister is dead? She's dead, she's gone, and that's that. Think of what you're going to do tomorrow."

Every member of Argentinita's company (except for Manolo Vargas, who was in Mexico when she died) acted as though her death were the greatest tragedy in the world. They all made out that they'd dearly loved Argentinita.

As far as I was concerned, it was all fraud. Secretly, they were happy to see her gone, or so I felt. Now Pilar had no rivals. She would be the star. Now Teresa had revenge for her unrequited love. If they or the others felt any real grief, I believed, it was because their provider was gone and they would now have to look after themselves.

Just before Argentinita had gone into the hospital, a famous Italian sculptor, Rosario Morabito (in Sicily, Rosario is a man's name), began to make a statue of Argentinita. It was unfinished at the time of her death. To help him complete it, Nila posed several times.

The finished statue looked like Argentinita, of course, but it also contained distinct hints of Nila—a symbolism that reflected what was going on inside me, in real life.

Part of me wanted to be with Nila, to continue our career together, to allow our love to flower. Another part of me wanted to stay with Argentinita, to accompany her body to Spain, to be with her when she was laid to rest.

There were other reasons for going to Spain, too. Since it was the source of my art, I felt I had to know it better. Argentinita had told me a great deal about the culture, but I wanted to experience it for myself.

So when Pilar announced that she was taking Argentinita's remains to Spain, I asked to go along, to spend a couple of months there. In a sense, I was undertaking a pilgrimage. I wanted to visit the shrine that I had worshiped from afar throughout my professional life.

It was important to me to make contact with the proud, beautiful, violent, passionate essence of Spain, perhaps to renew my devotion to it, or to make artistic communion.

Nila wasn't very happy that I was going, of course, but I assured her that I would return. Toward that end, I signed a contract engaging the William Morris agency to represent me during the 1946–47 season.

At the boat, Nila told me she had the feeling we'd never see each other again.

"That's nonsense," I assured her. "Things between us have just begun. You'll see."

I held out my hand, drew my ring off my finger—the ring Argentinita had given me in San Francisco, after we'd argued about a choreography, perhaps my most precious possession—and gave it to her.

Then Nila and I embraced and said good-bye.

ELEVEN

Pilar, her husband, and I—along with Argentinita's remains—arrived in Bilbao, Spain, on December 21, 1945. We'd brought with us a copy of Morabito's statue, the original taking a place at the Metropolitan Opera House in New York.

From there, Argentinita's body was taken to Madrid, under official auspices. The government, recognizing her contributions to the country, had decided to pay her public tribute and had arranged for her to lie in state.

I arrived in Madrid on December 23, my twenty-seventh birthday, and a miserable winter day. From there, I went to the Teatro Español, on a lovely downtown plaza, where Argentinita's body was on view.

All of Spain—it seemed to me—had turned out to pay its tribute to the great Argentinita. More than twenty-five thousand people filed past her open coffin.

Then, with an orchestra playing in front of the theater, the eulogies began. Many of Argentinita's eminent friends had come to offer their respects—Edgar Neville, Ortega y Gasset, Dr. Gregorio Maranon (Spain's most famous physician and philosopher), and a number of high governmental officials.

It was an extremely moving moment for me. Truly, Argentinita was home again, among those who loved her, among those she loved. The adulation Spain showed her that day had deep resonances within me, for it mirrored my feelings.

After the ceremonies, we accompanied the body to San Isidro cemetery, where Argentinita was at last laid to rest, in a beautiful Pantheon. Morabito's statue took its place there.

For several months after that, Pilar and I visited the cemetery daily, to pray, to leave flowers. I went because of the devotion I had to Argentinita's memory. Pilar, I believe, went seeking forgiveness for the way she'd treated her sister in the previous year or two. Her main motivation was guilt. At least that's the way I saw it.

And it was guilt that made her almost worshipful to me in this period. She nearly smothered me with affection, as if trying to make up —for Argentinita's sake—for the way she'd treated me in the past.

Over and over again, she told me I'd given Argentinita happiness in her last years, whatever else had happened. Of course, I never told her how deep our relationship had been. I wouldn't have dared, not then.

After a while, Edgar Neville came to me with an idea. He didn't want Argentinita's great art to perish with her death. He wanted Pilar to form a new company to carry on, to preserve for the Spanish people what Argentinita had created.

"Have you talked to Pilar about this?"

"Yes. But she's confused and bitter. She didn't want any part of it."

I understood all too well. Pilar must have felt that if she now formed her own company, she'd be doing exactly what she'd been threatening Argentinita with in their last year. Her conscience couldn't accept this.

"Edgar," I said, "I think your idea is wonderful. I'll do my best to convince Pilar to agree."

Later, I approached Pilar. I told her that her sister would have wanted her to continue, to preserve all that Argentinita had done. Because of how Pilar felt about me, because of how her sister had felt about me, she could accept this.

A few days later, Neville told me Pilar Lopez had agreed to form a company. Then she came to me.

"Of course, I want you to be in the company, José."

I sighed. "I understand, Pilar, and I am honored. But it is impossible. I have a contract with William Morris for the coming season. I must return to New York. I have a partner there, you know, Nila Amparo."

"Have her come here, José. We could use her in the company. She's a good dancer."

"But my contract . . ."

By now, Pilar was starting to get annoyed. "Your contract? What contract. I don't believe you."

"But it's true. Here, let me show you." I rummaged through my papers and came up with it. Pilar grabbed the document out of my hands and read the first page.

"You know what this is?" she asked, shaking with rage. "This is a lot of shit. That's all this is."

And she ripped it up and threw it away.

"Pilar, tearing it up doesn't make any difference. I still have to honor it."

"It's a lot of shit. It's phony."

She walked out before I could reply.

That night, I wrote the William Morris Agency. I asked them what sort of work they'd been able to find me and told them I'd like to stay in Spain a little longer, to prepare some new dances.

William Morris responded that they'd gotten me a few spot bookings—nothing that couldn't be put off if I wanted to stay in Spain a bit longer. So I joined Pilar's company. And I sent for Nila.

Nila arrived at Santander, on Spain's northern coast, in the middle of February. It was as if we'd never been apart. We rejoiced at seeing each other, had a few idyllic moments together, then boarded the train for Madrid.

The train trip wasn't very pleasant for either of us. Nila had eaten something that disagreed with her. She became violently ill, and there was no one to help except me. I did the best I could, but she was in bad shape when we arrived in Madrid. It took weeks before she was normal again.

"We do need another male dancer," Pilar said one night.

"What about Manolo?"

"You mean you want Manolo Vargas to join the company?"

"Of course. Why not? He's an excellent dancer. Besides, I know you want to present what Argentinita created. I think she created you and me and Manolo and the entire show. It wouldn't be the same without him."

"You're right, José. Let's send for Manolo."

That turned out to be easier said than done. Manolo was in Mexico, a country that had no governmental ties whatever with Spain, due to animosity springing from the Spanish Civil War.

"We need someone in America who's trustworthy and persistent, who can contact Manolo and make sure he's able to get here," Pilar said.

"I know just the man. He'll do *anything* for us."

"Fine. You arrange it."

I was thinking of Joaquin Pares, my old friend, the odd little man who'd made it clear he'd go to the ends of the earth for me. Joaquin was out of the Army, after a horrendous stint in the South Pacific that he barely survived, and was now living in New York.

Joaquin and Manolo arrived in Madrid in April. From that moment until his death, many years later, Joaquin remained associated with me.

Now the company was complete. Acting as unofficial company manager, as I had in the United States, I oversaw the making and design of our sets and costumes.

Then we began to rehearse, with opening day slightly more than two months away. I knew how American audiences reacted to our show, but I had no idea how it would be received here. This, after all, was Spain, this was Madrid.

The theater Edgar Neville had chosen for us was the marvelous Fontalba, on José Antonio Boulevard. The Fontalba is gone now, replaced by a large bank. But in its day, the Fontalba was one of the most beautiful theaters in Madrid, perhaps one of the most beautiful in all of Spain.

About eight-thirty on the night of June 6, 1946, the time for rehearsals was over. At that moment, the curtain rose on the Ballet Español. We had no idea how we would be received.

We found out after the first number. The standing-room-only audience burst out into thunderous applause. And it was the same after each number. When the show came to an end, we were kept on stage for many curtain calls.

The next morning, the newspapers were singing our praises. Everyone in the company was lauded, and I was singled out for special attention, "for bringing art back to the Spanish dance."

As a result of our Fontalba success, we soon found ourselves booked solid into the middle of 1947, in theaters all over Spain. We were to finish our run in Madrid (after a month and a half at the Fontalba), take a vacation during the six hottest weeks of the Spanish summer (when it was impossible to get anyone into a theater), then begin our tour.

During this period, Nila and I spent every possible moment together, of course. Our love blossomed. We had only one problem: As two single people, we could not live together with propriety, not in that city.

After we closed in Madrid in July, Nila and I sailed back to New

York to correct this oversight. For the immediate future, our careers were assured. It was now time to formalize our relationship.

In August 1946, Nila and I were married. Soon after, we returned to Spain to begin the new season, this time as husband and wife.

In September, we opened in San Sebastian, on Spain's northern coast, near the French border. Before our performance, during the day, there was the typical murmur that always occurs in cafes, bars, and restaurants that something great is about to happen, either in the bullring or in the theater.

It was in this environment that I ran into my dear friend Bob Kieve. Bob had been brought backstage at the end of a performance during our opening season at the Fontalba Theater by Arno Dosch-Fleurot (the Parisian correspondent for the *Christian Science Monitor* and an old friend) and was astonished to learn that I'd been born in Italy, raised in the United States, and spoke English as well as he did.

At the time, Bob was with the U. S. Embassy, and he was very much concerned with helping Spain's radio industry. He was helping one of Madrid's largest stations to design modern programming.

At any rate, Bob—who was and still is an aficionado of flamenco dancing—and I hit it off marvelously well. He, his girlfriend, Nila, and I went out two or three times a week to Madrid's most popular restaurants—places Like El Kiahon, which was one of Hemingway's favorites—then ending the evening at a Cafe Cantante, where real flamenco was performed. It was a great thing, having had Bob's advice, help, and friendship.

We met again in San Sebastian, where we rehashed the Madrid opening. Then we went out again, to the flamenco Cafe Cantante. Bob is an important man now, a resident of San José, California, and when we see each other, he helps me keep those early memories alive and stimulating.

San Sebastian was another remarkable success. And afterward we went on to Bilbao, Barcelona, Valencia, Saragossa, Salamanca, and Valladolid, all with the same result.

We crisscrossed Spain in every direction, eighteen performing artists, plus a symphony orchestra of perhaps thirty men, traveling on very comfortable trains, spending long hours in pleasant conversation.

Ahead of us, however, lay the ultimate test: Seville.

Seville is the home of flamenco dancing. It is the source. And the city proclaims this proudly: No flamenco dancer is truly a flamenco dancer until he has performed in Seville, until he has survived the scrutiny of those beside whom all others' knowledge pales.

I had been nervous before we opened in Madrid, but, on reflection, I had nothing to worry about. Given the populace's adulation of Argentinita, we could hardly have failed. But Seville was a different story altogether.

It was as if the city had been biding its time, waiting for us, waiting to see if we actually were what we claimed to be. They would inform us. Like wizened jewelers with loupes and magnifying eyeglasses, they knew the difference between the genuine article and the fake.

Our Ballet Español arrived in Seville late in November 1946. We went immediately to the theater to set up. I could feel the tension building. It was as if my performance tonight would determine, finally, whether or not this Italian kid from Brooklyn was a Spanish dancer.

As curtain time approached, the theater filled up rapidly. Every great flamenco artist in Seville, every critic, every expert—self-proclaimed or generally acknowledged—had come to see us. Were they here to recognize us or to humiliate us?

The lights dimmed and the curtain went up. All of a sudden, I found myself on stage, doing a solo, in the midst of the most crucial moment of my career. I did a movement and a break, and another movement. Summoning all of my fervor, I threw myself into my dance with all of my being.

I began to realize that the audience was making some sort of noise. It was shouting. It was yelling rhythmically. Slowly, it dawned on me what the audience was saying.

With each of my movements, it was crying out, "¡Olé! ¡Olé!"

When I finished, the applause was deafening. They would not let me leave the stage. Once more, I began. I repeated myself, with even more fervor than before, if that were possible.

And once more, the entire theater accompanied me, the building reverberating with the roar of "¡Olé! ¡Olé! ¡Olé!" I was dumfounded. Was I dreaming? Was this truly possible?

Finally they let me leave the stage, but only after thunderous applause, applause of the sort a performer only dreams of hearing. It was total approval, complete and undiluted. It was nothing less than adulation.

I found Pilar in the wings.

"Did you hear that? They shouted '*Olé.*' Is that the custom here?"

"No, José. There is no such custom, not here, not anywhere. '*Olé*' is a word reserved for bullfighters, for men who demonstrate perfect grace at the instant they face death."

"But surely other dancers . . ."

"No. Never. Never in my experience, never to my knowledge."

It was a fluke, I told myself. It was the dance, the choreography, the costumes, the settings, or the combination. A while later, I went back out on stage for another solo, fully expecting a far more temperate reaction.

"*¡Olé! ¡Olé! ¡Olé!*" It was as if the audience too had rehearsed and was shouting out its approbation at the command of a director. It was a miracle. Or maybe I had died without knowing it and gone to heaven.

Once more I was forced to repeat my dance, and once again the audience cheered. I was Caesar, I was Einstein, I was Paderewsky, I was Heifetz, I was Toscanini, I was Picasso, I was Nijinsky. I was transported into realms beyond my wildest dreams.

I did not sleep that night. I waited for the morning papers, to find out if I had correctly perceived reality. The critics responded to me exactly as the audience had—they applied every known laudatory adjective: fabulous, fantastic, stupendous, marvelous, etc.

And they, like I, could not get over how the audience had cheered me. "Never before has an audience honored a dancer by shouting out '*¡Olé!*' but Greco fully deserved the bullfighter's accolade. Never have I seen such grace, such dancing, at precisely the moment when his performance first came under Sevillian scrutiny. Greco has not only brought art, true art, back to Spanish dancing, he has also brought manhood!"

It was then that I told a newspaper interviewer of my Italian birth and Brooklyn upbringing, only to have him scoff, both in person and in print. "Greco says he was born in Italy," the man wrote, "but this cannot be. Anyone who has seen him dance knows he must be the product of generations of Spaniards."

The truth is, I was closer, both in body and spirit, to my Italian origins than I had been in twenty years—since I'd sailed for America. Italy was just a short boat ride away, and Montorio just across the "boot."

I felt myself longing to see my home again, longing to renew old acquaintances. I wanted once more to shake the hand of the priest who had comforted me when I'd eaten that lump of sugar. I even wanted to see the "sinister" carpenter, to vanquish that nightmare. I wanted to see my aunts and uncles and cousins.

This was the time, you may remember, of *Open City* and *The Bicycle Thief*. Italy had just gone through a devastating war, drawn into the Nazi orbit by a foolish man who did not know his limitations. The country had been the scene of great struggles between opposing armies.

My mother had been getting letters from relatives in Montorio, describing the travail they'd gone through. There'd been no actual fighting in or around Montorio, but the town was suffering from shortages of all kinds. Food, clothing, and other essentials of life were in pitifully short supply, my relatives wrote. Such simple necessities as black pepper were unobtainable.

As I danced my way through Spain, I determined to return to Montorio. What's more, I determined to share with my kinsmen and townsfolk the proceeds of my good fortune. They lacked food, clothing, spices, and other essentials? Then I would bring them what they needed.

Toward that end, I saved a great deal from the money Pilar paid me. But I could never seem to save enough. One reason, I felt, was that I wasn't being paid my due. Seville had established what I'd thought before: that I was nearly as great a drawing card as Pilar herself, perhaps greater.

At the time I was getting three hundred pesetas a day and Nila was being paid two hundred pesetas a day, a total of five hundred pesetas. At the current exchange rate of twenty-five pesetas to the dollar, that was about twenty dollars a day—good money, but hardly adequate for a performer of my popularity.

And besides my popularity, there was also the matter of the extra work I was doing. Pilar was the boss, perhaps, but I was the chief. I had to do most of the choreography, the costuming, the lighting, the staging. There was no one else.

At the time, Pilar was clearing—after salaries to the company and the orchestra, after the theater's percentage—about three thousand dollars a day. Of course, I wanted more money. But I also wanted recognition of my stature.

Pilar wasn't interested in doing that. Not at all. In this period of her life, anyhow, she mistreated people terribly, as anyone who was with her can testify. She had a way of making you feel small and insignificant. I didn't like that. I didn't feel she had any right to treat me that way. Thus began a long series of bitter arguments.

For now, though, she began to pay me more, enough so that I was able to save nearly eight thousand dollars. This was my Montorio fund. With this money, I was going to buy my birthplace the goods it needed to recover from the war.

In the spring of 1947, I sent my parents to Montorio—they'd always hoped to visit—to see friends and relatives, to ready the town for my visit that summer.

Meanwhile, I collected goods to bring to my *paisanos*, eventually spending everything I'd saved. I bought clothing, textiles, hats, shoes, enough to dress half the village from winter through summer. I bought gifts for everyone. I made a special trip to Tangiers and bought ten kilos of black pepper for my aunt, who couldn't get any in Montorio.

I longed to do all I could for my friends and relatives. More than that, I longed to see my past, to return to that wonderfully innocent period of my youth where everything was green pastures and cloudless skies, to see old acquaintances whose names and faces were only dim memories.

That year, 1947, our tour ended in June in Barcelona, on Spain's southern coast, a perfect point of departure for Italy. By that time, I'd accumulated twenty theatrical trunks filled with goods of every description.

After our last performance in Barcelona, I had those trunks loaded aboard a boat, and Nila and I set sail for Genoa. I was going home.

TWELVE

At Barcelona, customs officials had cast a curious eye at my twenty theatrical trunks. "It's costumes and sets," I told them. "We'll be performing in Italy." Since we were leaving the country—not entering—they gave us no trouble.

I'd written ahead to my mother to be sure Nila and I were met in Genoa. I'd sent her money to rent a truck (to carry the trunks back to Montorio) and a bus, for those uncles, aunts, and cousins who wanted to meet us at the boat.

The trip itself was uneventful, but I found myself in trouble soon after I disembarked. Italian customs officials were astounded by my twenty enormous trunks and the bounty with which they were filled.

"What *is* all this stuff?" one official asked.

"Gifts. Gifts for my relatives."

"Gifts? You must be joking. Don't try to hand me that. You're a black marketeer—that's obvious."

"No, no," I protested. "I just have lots of relatives."

"Of course."

I looked beyond the customs line, to where my mother and my other relatives were waiting for Nila and me, waving and calling to us. "There they are—look for yourself!"

The customs official looked suspiciously at my reception committee. Then he turned back to me.

"Tell me, Signore Greco, have you any cigarettes?"

Our eyes met and locked.

"No," I said, "no cigarettes. But maybe this will make up for that."

I reached into my pocket and pulled out two hundred thousand lire—well over one hundred dollars. He accepted the cash and waved me through the line. "Have a nice stay in Italy, Signore Greco. And my regards to the relatives."

"Of course."

My uncles, my cousins, and I loaded the huge trunks onto the rented truck, all the relatives piled into the bus, and Nila, my parents, and I got into a car. For the next day, we drove the nearly three hundred miles from Genoa to Montorio, south and east across the Italian peninsula—bus, car, and truck together in a little caravan.

As we approached Montorio, we came to a little crossroads. In one direction was the famous St. Michael fountain and another small community. In the other was the place of my birth.

Well, the entire town had come down to this crossroads to meet us, including the town band. It was one of the most incredible moments of my life, with the band playing, people crying, everyone embracing.

Together now, the caravan, swelled by the addition of most of Montorio's population, proceeded into the town itself, to the plaza in the center of the village, the plaza where I'd played as a child more than twenty years earlier.

Now everyone got out of the car and the bus and I began to look at everyone, and everyone looked familiar to me. They started to come up to me, timidly at first—I was now the rich and famous dancer—then with more assurance.

"Hey, Costanzo, do you know who I am?"

"Of course I know who you are."

"Then who am I?"

The faces were familiar, but how could I possibly recall the names? I hadn't been in Montorio since I was eight years old.

"You're from Montorio, aren't you?"

"Yeah, but what's my name?"

"Uh, you're Antonio."

"Eh? No, no, I'm Giuseppe."

"Oh, I'm sorry, Giuseppe. Of course, you're Giuseppe. I just got confused for a moment."

This went on constantly, day after day, until every member of the community had tested my memory (and, in most cases, found it wanting). It even goes on now, with former associates or people from my distant past. Sometimes the people are those I could never forget, other times people I wouldn't have remembered for ten minutes—whether I was a nobody or the most famous person in the world. But this is how people are.

Anyhow, it was a beautiful experience in that plaza, to see the joy in my mother's face, to watch my relatives rejoicing, to see the entire town celebrating my return and my accomplishments.

Finally, we pulled the trunks down off the truck—right there in the plaza—and I opened them up. All of my relatives and their friends crowded around and oohed and ahhed over the trunks' contents.

"Go ahead," I said. "It's yours. I brought all of this stuff for you. Take!"

And they did. They began pulling things out of the trunks—suits, hats, shoes, bolts of textiles, coats, shawls.

"Look at this!" Someone would say, throwing a bolt of cloth into the air, unfurling it to the sky. "It's beautiful!"

"Which color shirt looks better on me, the white or the brown?"

"Has anyone found shoes of a big size?"

"How do I look in this?"

"I have one green sock—who has the other?"

"I will make a beautiful dress out of this, a dress for my daughter."

"How about this coat, this will keep you warm for the winter."

It was as if Montorio's plaza had been transformed into a scene from the *Arabian Nights*, as if the merchants in a bazaar had all departed, after telling their customers to choose whatever they wanted, no charge.

All of the goods I'd brought with me from Spain were now spread out over the plaza's rough paving blocks, or piled on the stone stoops of the houses, or they'd found owners, who'd put them on.

It was a beautiful, wonderful scene, well worth the money it had cost me, well worth the trouble. The childlike happiness that glowed from the faces of my relatives and their friends had made it all worthwhile.

Wherever I looked, I saw joy. The people had needed, and I had brought. There were goodies for all—even for my aunt, who'd complained she was unable to buy black pepper.

During the trip from Barcelona to Montorio, some of the boxes of black pepper—I'd bought ten kilos (twenty-two pounds) of it, you'll remember—had broken open in the trunks. (And, for many years, the trunks smelled of black pepper—some still do.) But enough was intact—more than enough.

"What am I going to do with all of this black pepper?" my aunt asked me.

"Didn't you want me to buy you black pepper?"

"Yes, of course, a little jar of it if it wasn't too much trouble—but ten kilos?"

In my eagerness to be generous, I'd made a mistake. I'd brought an overabundance. Not just of black pepper, of everything. I thought I was providing my kinsmen and their friends with what they needed. The truth was somewhat different.

After the initial excitement was over and I had a chance to sit down with everyone and get reacquainted, I found out that the war hadn't affected Montorio in anything like the way it had affected many other parts of Italy.

"It was all parties, Costanzo," one uncle told me. "The Germans came through and they gave big parties in Montorio. Then the Americans came through and they gave big parties. Then the English came through and they gave big parties."

"But what about the fighting? What about the war?"

"What war?"

"You mean nobody ever got hurt?"

"With a bullet? With a bayonet? Of course not."

"Of course not?"

"We watched the whole thing through binoculars, Costanzo. One time a German came and told us he was going to be the commander and maintain order. Then he disappeared and the Americans came and said the same thing. Then the British came and they said the same. There was no war here."

"What about the letters you wrote Mama, when you talked about the shortages and the struggle and the horrible things that happened? What did that mean?"

My uncle sighed painfully. "Ah, Costanzo, you have to understand. Everybody in Italy was writing letters like that to his relatives in America. We felt we had to do the same, so we didn't make liars of the others. We felt we had to maintain the image. Perhaps we felt that was what you wanted to hear."

"Then all the things I brought . . ."

"You're so generous with us, Costanzo."

"But you really didn't need . . ."

"We could always use such things. We were never rich, you know. But, next time . . ."

"Next time what?"

"Well, money would be more useful. With money, we could buy our own goods, cheaper than you could buy them."

"I see."

"Understand, Costanzo, we're very grateful, all of us. It was a wonderful thing you did."

"Perhaps."

"It's just that . . ."

"I understand, uncle, I understand truly."

I understood all too well.

I did give out some money, in addition to the clothing and the goods. In fact, I gave my uncle enough money to buy the truck he wanted. Eventually, he sold it because he didn't know how to drive and he didn't want to learn.

Since that time, I've often returned to Montorio—not with trunks, but with cash, in response to stories of need, so as not to disappoint. And I've wondered how my friends and relatives in Montorio would respond if I came empty-handed.

Looking back, I wonder now if I did a good thing, bringing all of those trunks full of merchandise. I wonder if I really helped these people in any important way. I think not.

I may even have hurt them, leading them to believe they could count on such benevolences from time to time, leading them to become dependent, leading them to exaggerate their needs—to lie, leading them to feel they deserved such treatment, as a matter of course.

Perhaps this is true of all small, somewhat isolated communities, but the people of Montorio are a very prideful, very jealous group. They refuse to believe—perhaps because they sense the truth—that they are any less sophisticated, any less educated, any less well-dressed than, say, the elite of New York society.

I remember, on that first trip back, having a typical conversation of this kind with Antonio, my oldest male cousin, then about eighteen. He looked at me and said, "Hey, you're not wearing a tie."

I laughed. "No. I'm not going to wear a tie in Montorio. I mean, let's face it."

"But if you were to wear a tie, how do you put it on? I'm curious."

"I'll show you, if you like."

I took a tie from my suitcase and, while he watched, slipped it around my neck and knotted it.

"Of course. That's right. You're from Montorio. You know how to knot a tie."

"What do you mean, Antonio?"

"Well, a couple of people passed through Montorio a while back —from Mexico or Argentina, I don't remember which—and they didn't even know how to knot a tie! They were hicks, that's all they were."

Eventually, my visits to Montorio became an annual event. And other emigrants also returned to see their old hometown. Finally, Montorio created a special celebration to mark this, the annual Feast of Pannochi, marking the harvesting of wheat and corn.

Every year now, the people of Montorio have their Feast of Corn, and they honor those who have gone out into the world, made names for themselves, and brought honor to Montorio.

A few years ago, I was the guest of honor at such a celebration, receiving a plaque for my contributions to Montorio's fame. It is an odd result of some misguided generosity.

Nila and I stayed in Montorio on that visit for nearly two months. Finally the time drew near when I had to leave my hometown and go back to Spain, to start my new season with Pilar Lopez and the Ballet Español.

Before I left, my mother told me she was going to buy me a present, a special present—a car.

"Don't spend so much money on me, Mama. Don't get me anything too fancy."

At this time—1947—new cars were unobtainable in Italy. Not until 1949 would that country amaze the world with beautiful new Alfa Romeos, Maseratis, and Ferraris.

But my mother, remembering my request not to spend too much money, found me a used Fiat 1100, a nice little five-passenger car. Unfortunately, it wasn't in such good condition. The tires, particularly, were badly worn.

Nila and I decided to wait until the last possible moment to leave Montorio—August 8. We were to open in San Sebastian, on Spain's northern coast, on August 11. We figured it would take us twenty-four hours—or less—to drive there. That would give us at least two days to rest and rehearse.

Of course, we knew we were cutting things a little close, but in the peace and quiet of Montorio, it seemed like we could make it easily enough. At least that's what we thought.

We started out on the morning of the eighth, after a typical Italian breakfast and some typical Italian embraces. Before we had gone a hundred kilometers, we had a blowout. Somehow we got it fixed and continued.

After another hour or so, we had another flat. This one we also had repaired. But it wasn't very long after this that we had a third tire go bad.

We arrived in France in the dead of night. We made it through Marseilles and onto a small town called Sete. Then—bang!—another blowout. I don't know how I managed to maintain control of the car, but I did.

Continuing on, however, was out of the question. We'd long ago put on our spare (and tossed out the tire it replaced). There were no service stations open at that hour. And, given the shortages, it was very unlikely I would have been able to find the right-sized tire, even if they had been open.

Fortunately, there was an American Army base nearby. A GI helped me jack up the car, and he found some kind of wheel back at the base—not the right size, but close enough. Nila and I drove into Sete, where we spent the night.

I was up at six-thirty the next morning—we were already behind schedule—searching for a tire so that we could keep going. I finally located a man who had one and was willing to sell it—at only four times the normal price. But what choice did I have?

Off we went again, considerably the worse for wear. We headed northwest, toward Toulouse, Tarbes, and Pau. And we ran into the most incredible deluge I'd ever seen—a wall of rain that turned the windshield practically opaque.

Suddenly I couldn't go more than twenty or thirty miles an hour —and that was taking chances. On and on we went through the rain, without sleep, along flooded roads that weren't that good when they were dry.

The trip from Sete to San Sebastian was a nightmare. I desperately wanted to arrive in time for the performance. Yet no matter how hard I tried, we fell farther and farther behind schedule.

By now there was no question of having a day or two to rest and rehearse. I just wanted to get to the theater before the curtain went up. Toward this end, I drove myself with all of my strength and energy.

We went through Biarritz at about seven at night—two hours before I was due to perform in San Sebastian, which was less than thirty miles' distant. It began to look as though I'd make it.

Then we hit the French-Spanish border—and customs. I don't know why, but the customs officials took this occasion to search our luggage so carefully they must have thought we were diamond smugglers.

While they searched, I paced and swore under my breath. Every minute they took was a minute I couldn't spend rushing toward the theater. Finally they finished. Nila and I jumped into the car and drove off. It was now seven forty-five.

We pulled up in front of the theater a bare half hour before curtain time and we rushed through the stage door. Nila and I were both exhausted and distraught, but ready to do what was required of us.

No one was there, not in the dressing rooms, not sitting in the orchestra, waiting for the curtain to go up. In fact, besides Nila and myself, the only human being in the theater was the night watchman.

For reasons I could not comprehend, the performance had been canceled.

THIRTEEN

We got back into the car again and went off to search for Pilar Lopez—and for an explanation. We found her at her hotel.

"There you are! Now you show up! Where were you, you son-of-a-bitch?"

"I had troubles on the road, Pilar. There was nothing I could do. Even so, I was there, at the theater, a half hour before curtain time. But the show was canceled. I can't understand this—why was it canceled?"

"You were there? Why couldn't you have called us from the road? Why couldn't you have told us you were going to make it?"

"I didn't know I was going to make it until I did. Anyhow, there was no time to call. We had four flat tires and we went through the most incredible rain—I haven't slept in forty-eight hours," I told Pilar.

"That means nothing to me, you bastard. You've cost us thousands of pesetas, and you'll pay," she shouted. "You'll pay back every centimo!"

"What do you mean, I've cost you? And why was the performance canceled?"

Pilar looked at me imperiously, her face filled with scorn and derision. "Because of you, you idiot! Because you stayed in Italy eating pasta and acting the big hero. Because we didn't know when—or whether—we'd ever see you again."

"But Pilar, I've never missed a performance in my life. Not one."

"Hah!"

"You mean the Ballet Español canceled its performance because I didn't show up? With a company of eighteen dancers and thirty musicians, you couldn't go on if *I* didn't show up?"

Pilar immediately understood the implications of my question. If I were the indispensable performer, what was she? If the show couldn't go on without me, what did that say about my importance to the company?

"It's the law in Spain. If one of the announced performers in a show cannot appear, the company may postpone the performance."

I had to smile at that one. "That's bullshit, Pilar—and you know it. You can always make the announcement just before the curtain goes up and give the audience a chance either to stay or leave and get a refund. You know what almost always happens then—they all stay."

"You're a fool and you're irresponsible, José. And you've cost the company twenty thousand pesetas because of your unforgiveable behavior. You're going to pay it all back."

This didn't bother me very much. If it took twenty thousand pesetas to convince Pilar that I should hold a coequal position with her in the company, so be it. Maybe I should have felt ashamed at what I'd done, not keeping in touch. But all I felt was pride—pride that the show couldn't open without *me*.

It was in this atmosphere that the Ballet Español began its 1947–48 season. The animosity between Pilar and myself was growing, but so was my power and my stature.

We opened the next day in San Sebastian, then once more toured Spain by train, hitting many of the cities in which we'd performed the year before, adding others.

And before and after these performances—even sometimes during —Pilar and I argued. I felt my contributions to the Ballet Español were such that I was entitled to enjoy the image of José Greco *and* Pilar Lopez or Pilar Lopez *and* José Greco and *their* Ballet Español. She insisted that she was the only star and that the ballet was hers and hers alone.

I didn't feel that I was merely another member of the company. I felt that people came to see our show in large part, at least, because I was in it. I wanted my contributions recognized. It was a matter of pride, but it was also a matter of security. I didn't want her to feel she could fire me whenever the mood struck her.

But nothing I could say or do seemed to move the woman. It was the Ballet Español of Pilar Lopez, she said, and that's the way it would always be. She would never yield to me.

Yet now she did begin to yield to me, at least to a degree. By the

93

time the previous season had ended, she'd raised my salary to fifteen hundred pesetas a day. And after we played the San Carlos theater in Lisbon, Portugal, and I once more stopped the show again and again, I demanded—and got—fifteen hundred pesetas for *each* performance, or three thousand pesetas a day (we did two shows daily).

In this period, Nila was no longer performing with the Ballet Español, because of health problems. She came down with an intestinal parasite that steadily sapped her strength. Eventually, she was put under a doctor's care. He allowed her to rehearse, but forbade travel. So I performed with the company on my own.

There are some people, I've found, who constantly suffer from illnesses or accidents, who are forever involved with medicine and doctors and hospitals. Melba Peters—Nila's mother—was one of these. And, as time passed, I began to think that Nila might have inherited this tendency.

This disturbed me greatly. Nila was my wife, and I cared for her deeply. But I was uncomfortable with what I saw as her weakness, her overdependence. This manifested itself not only physically, but also emotionally. It did not threaten our relationship—there was no one else in my life—but it kept me from being as close to her as I would have wanted.

As for Pilar, I did everything I could think of to convince her to accept me not as an employee, but as a partner. First, I tried to persuade her, citing the audiences and the critics. Then I threatened. I told her I'd quit and form my own company if she didn't grant me the status I deserved.

Both tactics had no effect. She was the star and her company was based on her sister's choreographies. Male dancers? They were interchangeable. As for my quitting, she made out that she didn't give two hoots in hell whether I stayed with the company or went my own merry way.

But the case I'd made for myself was not so easy to dismiss. It rankled her so that she looked for some way—any way—to show me who the audiences really came to see, to prove that I wasn't such hot stuff.

In the spring of 1948, we returned to the scene of my greatest triumph—Seville. I don't know whether or not she consciously planned it, but it was obvious she hoped to humiliate me here.

On our opening night, Pilar went out and did a solo number that truly brought down the house. The applause was so overwhelming the entire building shook. She flounced off the stage—between bows —and found me standing in the wings.

"So! You think *I* need you, do you? Well, listen. Then you'll know just who needs whom!"

She went back out on stage and took some more bows. The applause was incredible. The audience whistled and stamped its feet. And I listened.

Off the stage she came again. "Do you hear them, José? That's how they respond to a *star!*"

It would have been all right, perhaps, if her arrogance had been without foundation. But how could I deny the evidence of my ears? It was the kind of recognition that is rarely heard in any theater.

She took another bow, then came off and twitted me once more. "Remember, that applause is for Pilar López, not some upstart named José Greco!"

I had to admit to myself that she was speaking the truth. Perhaps she was right. Perhaps she was the star of the greatest magnitude. I was glum as I waited in the wings for my own number.

After I don't know how many bows, Pilar came off the stage and swept by me as if I were nothing more than a stagehand, her face radiant with triumph. She headed for her dressing room, leaving me there to ruminate.

There was some kind of number between her solo and mine. While it was on, I hung around the wings and tried to compose myself. I knew what I had to do, if I were to survive, if I were to retain any self-esteem.

Then, almost without warning, it was my turn.

I went out on stage. And I began to dance. I summoned forth all of my art. I gave of myself as I had never given before, without restraint, with no thought of what might come next.

And then I heard it again: "*¡Olé! ¡Olé! ¡OLÉ! ¡¡OLÉ!!*" They remembered me. Once more, they honored me with that sacrosanct cry of approbation reserved for the bullfighter as he does his passes with the bull, when the risk of death is greatest.

When I finished my number, the audience literally went insane. The cheering and screaming and yelling and stamping of feet was simply not to be believed. I thought the theater, like the walls of Jericho, might come tumbling down.

I took a bow and left the stage. Then I returned and took another and another. But the noise didn't diminish. If anything, it increased and swelled in volume. It was completely beyond belief. I had danced and produced some kind of mass hysteria.

Now, with the noise shaking the walls of the theater, I walked back to Pilar's dressing room and knocked on the door.

An angry voice responded. "Who is it?"

"It's me, Pilar—José."

"José! Why aren't you on stage, taking your bow?"

"I just want you to know that the show can't go on unless I go and take some more bows, that's all."

There was no response.

"Pilar? Are you listening to me? The show isn't going to go on until I go back out there and take more bows. The audience won't let it."

The door opened abruptly. Pilar stood there, red-faced and furious. "So? Why are you telling me this?"

I smiled back. "Well, I just wanted you to know how much you need *me*. You said you didn't need me. Shall I go and bow, or shall I stay here?"

She stared at me for what seemed like a full minute. And all the while, the applause was deafening. We had to shout to make ourselves heard.

Then she whirled and slammed the door in my face—boom!

I shrugged my shoulders, went back out on stage, and did the encore the audience was demanding. Once more, they responded as if I'd just given them the secret of eternal life. And once more, after taking a couple of bows, I trotted backstage to Pilar's dressing room and knocked on the door.

"Who wants me?"

"It's José again, Pilar. I don't know what to do, Pilar. They're still applauding. What should I do now?"

Dead silence.

Not long afterward, we were approached by the Spanish attaché to France. At the time, Franco's government was recognized by only a few countries—the result of the bitterness over the Spanish Civil War.

But France was beginning to liberalize her policies toward Spain. France wanted to re-establish its relationship with its neighbor to the west, albeit gradually, through cultural exchanges.

Spain's official representative to France, the attaché, had suggested that this exchange begin with a trip to Paris by the Ballet Español.

He felt our company could provide a perfect beginning to a renewed friendship.

When I heard of his offer, I again approached Pilar with my demands.

"The company must be the joint undertaking of both Pilar Lopez *and* José Greco, and it must be billed that way," I told her.

"Impossible," she snapped back. "I won't have it."

"Then you won't have me, Pilar."

"What do you mean?"

"If you don't agree to my terms, we're finished. I won't go to Paris with you. And after this season ends, I'll leave the company."

Pilar was livid with rage. "I'll never agree to your terms, you son-of-a-bitch. Who do you think you are, you bastard? You're a worm, that's all you are! You were a worm when my sister took pity on you, and that's what you'll be if you leave me. Besides, who needs you, you worm? I can replace you in an instant."

"Well, then, that's what you'll have to do, because I'm going to go my own way and do what I have to do."

"Then you're a fool and an idiot. You'll come back to me someday and beg on your fucking knees to get a job from me. And when you do, I'll tell you to go stuff your head up your ass!"

I sighed. "Well, when that day comes, Pilar, I suppose I'll have to live with whatever happens. But now I cannot continue to dance with you."

Pilar told the Spanish attaché that the Ballet Español would be more than delighted to perform in Paris. José Greco wouldn't be performing, but that wasn't important, she could get someone else just as good. The Spanish attaché decided that under those conditions, maybe it was best that the Ballet Español didn't go to France.

Now, people began to plead with me to stay with Pilar. The first was Adrian Izquierdo, her personal manager and impresario.

"Don't leave the company, José," he said. "If you do, Pilar's days as an economically viable performer are numbered. She'd manage a few years on her own, and that will be the end of it."

Sure enough, that was exactly what happened. Fortunately for her, when her drawing ability had shriveled up to almost nothing, the Spanish Government stepped in with subsidies. Even then, she had to people her company with fourth-rate dancers in order to survive. She cannot deny this; the truth is there for all to see.

Later, Argentinita's famous friends came to me, one by one, to ask me to stay with the Ballet Español. I heard from them all: Edgar Neville, Dr. Maranon, Ortega y Gasset, Sir Walter Starkey, José Maria Cossio, and many others.

I told them all the same thing: I was sorry, but there were some things I just could not help doing, and this was one of them. Perhaps I had to find my own way. I hoped that, regardless of what happened, I would somehow make them proud of me.

As summer approached and the 1947–48 season drew to a close, I began to put together my own little company of Spanish dancers. At its core were Nila—now better—and myself.

To this core was added Luis Olivares (Nila's brother), an older woman he'd known in America named Carola Goya, and Norina, my sister—not there to perform, of course, but to lend her support and to be part of the family.

I also hired Joaquina Marti, one of Pilar's pianists, to be my musical director, and her husband, Diego, to be our stage and property manager. But Joaquina did not leave Pilar until I'd actually stopped performing with the Ballet Español.

It was my thought that Nila would take on those roles played by Argentinita in the old days, while Luis would take the part of Manolo Vargas. Carola Goya, a classic dancer, would add her own element.

In addition, I would find a gypsy couple somewhere in Spain and perhaps half a dozen or a dozen other secondary dancers, depending on the talent available and the money I had to spend.

As for the music and the choreography—well, there's a little of the thief in all of us, and I guess I'm no exception. Without telling her why, I asked Joaquina Marti to let me see the Ballet Español scores she was working with.

"How come?" she asked.

"Oh, well, you know, so that I can make copies, in case they're needed."

"No problem, José."

When she gave me the scores, I photographed them with my new Bolex movie camera, a frame at a time, a page at a time. This seemed to me the fastest and cheapest way to outfit my own company with the scores it needed.

But when I took the film to the camera shop and told them that I wanted it enlarged, frame by frame, I found out that the cost was astronomical. I ended up getting the musical arrangements from conventional sources, above-board.

The dance choreographies were another matter. I felt I could use any of those I'd helped to develop. I also felt that I had a right to use those choreographies devised by Argentinita—so long as I gave her credit. After all, wasn't that exactly what Pilar Lopez was doing?

All artists, in a sense, build on the art of those who went before them. I was building on the art of Argentinita and Carmen Amaya and Vicente Escudero and the many great dancers who had preceded them.

Did Pilar own what Argentinita had created? There was nothing in Argentinita's will to that effect. As far as I was concerned, I had as much right to these things as Pilar did—particularly those she didn't use, or those I had to rework or reconstruct.

As far as Pilar was concerned, of course, my use of these routines was just one more excuse to call me a bastard or a son-of-a-bitch. I'm not saying I was guiltless here, but I am saying the issue wasn't as black-and-white as Pilar wanted to make out.

Anyhow, I wasn't the only trickster. Pilar wasn't above pulling off one of her own. Totally without my knowledge—so she thought— she arranged to hire a replacement for me, a Mexican dancer named Ximinez, a friend of Manolo Vargas's.

There was only one leak in her security system—and it was a doozy: She'd had my devoted friend Joaquin Pares make the arrangements for Ximinez to leave Mexico and travel directly to Spain, just as he had arranged Manolo's trip two years earlier. Joaquin kept me completely informed.

At this time, I was putting my own company together and rehearsing them in the theater at which the Ballet Español was playing— with the theater's permission. In a few weeks, the season would be over and my company and I would be on our own.

To tell the truth, we had very little going for us at the time, except my optimism—and some well-told lies. I'd put my company together—at least those members not in the "family"—by telling them that I had offers from all over Europe. I didn't have any offers. None. But I had hopes.

One day, while we were rehearsing—to be sure we'd be ready, when and if those hopes materialized—a young man, a stranger, walked into the theater, put his suitcase down, got into practice clothing, and started to rehearse.

"Excuse me," I said, "but the stage is occupied, by me and my group."

"Well, I was given orders to rehearse here and I don't know who you are, but I'm going to rehearse."

"I have news for you. Do you see that suitcase?"

"Yes. It's mine."

"Exactly. Pick it up right now and take it out the door."

"Wait a minute—who are you?"

"That doesn't matter. The only thing that matters is that I'm the boss here until someone tells me otherwise."

And that was my first enounter with Mr. Ximinez. Later, when he did join Pilar's company, he turned out to be totally unsuited for my roles.

The Ballet Español arrived in Barcelona in May 1948 for their last engagement of the season. I was coming to the end of another chapter in my life, but my mind was occupied with what lay ahead.

How was I going to continue to support Nila, Luis, Carola, Joaquin, Norina, and myself? How was I going to hold my company together, without work? Had I doomed myself by resigning from the Ballet Español? Was Pilar right—would I come back to her, begging for a job?

FOURTEEN

In one sense—the artistic one—I was confident I was ready to head up my own dance company. After all, I'd studied with the best teachers, worked with the most celebrated dancers, played to the most demanding audiences. Though I was not quite thirty, I'd had fifteen years of dance experience.

And in these last two years in Spain, I'd continued to study and perfect my art in every way I could. I'd visited just about every dance studio in the country, watched literally hundreds of unknown gypsies and folk artists to whom the dance was native.

I'd taken what I saw and blended it into my own art, practicing by myself for hours, then joining the Ballet Español's rehearsals. Finally, after our performances on stage, I'd often danced until dawn at flamenco parties that—underneath their festivity—were deadly serious contests of skill and endurance.

In another sense—the business one—I wasn't so sure of myself. Was I really ready to become my company's chief booking agent, to arrange season-long tours, to negotiate contracts, to provide the motive force for two dozen artists, to generate the income needed to support them?

To be sure, I knew (at least technically) how to do these things. What I hadn't done myself, I'd seen done. But I wasn't certain I had the personal contacts and the management expertise I needed to start a new company from scratch. That, however, was exactly what I was attempting to do.

What I needed now, more than anything else, was hard cash. My job with Pilar was ending, but my responsibility for the six people who made up my "family" in Spain was just beginning.

One day, while I was performing with the Ballet Español in Barcelona, an impresario stopped by to see me. "I understand you're looking for something new," he said. "Would you be interested in playing at a local night club for a week, sharing top billing with a famous Mexican singer?"

"What does the job pay?"

"A thousand dollars a day—six thousand dollars, total."

I could hardly believe my ears. This was more than I'd earned with Pilar in six months. And it involved no expenses, no guitarist. It was all profit.

"Well, I think I can do it."

I took my "family" back to Madrid and set them up in an apartment, then returned to Barcelona. The night club that had engaged me—the Cortijo—turned out to be a very swanky place indeed. Perhaps this might be a new direction for me, I thought. Certainly the money was there.

When evening approached, the time came to perform. When I stepped out onto the stage, the night club was packed. Its patrons were eating and drinking, but I tried not to let that bother me. At a thousand dollars a day, I told myself, you can overlook many things.

I began my dance. The audience responded almost immediately, applauding loudly, shouting "Bravo, Bravo." But I could hear other sounds that bothered me.

"Hey, Greco, you've got a great ass, you know that?"

"What are you doing after the show, Greco?"

"Look at the body on that guy!"

They were making personal comments to me, comments I found insulting and degrading. There had been none of this in the theater. There had been no drinking or eating during the performance, either.

I hadn't spent fifteen years bringing authenticity and purity to my art for this purpose. Even if I deserved no respect, what I was doing demanded it. And that it could never get in this sort of atmosphere.

Of course, I finished out my week at the Cortijo. But I knew that I could never again perform as a soloist in a night club, or while people ate and drank. I took my six thousand dollars and headed back to Madrid.

Temporarily, I was in good shape. But I had to make new plans quickly. With the number of mouths I had to feed, that six thousand dollars wouldn't last forever.

Again, luck stepped in.

I was buying some socks in a Madrid haberdashery when a total stranger called out my name.

"José Greco! Where the hell have you been? We've been searching for you all over Spain!"

"Looking for me? Why?"

"Well, I'm producing a movie about the famous bullfighter Manolete. The director and I have decided that you'd be the perfect person to play the young novice always looking forward to taking his place."

"Me? Act?" It seemed like complete nonsense. "How much does it pay?"

"Well, we also want a big dance scene, with hundreds of guitarists and hundreds of dancers . . ."

"Hundreds? Eh, calm down, calm down. What did you say it paid?"

"We'll pay you a hundred thousand pesetas."

Now that was a lot of money in those days—more than I'd made in the Barcelona night club. The whole thing sounded crazy, but what right did I have to complain?

"How long will you need me?"

"A month, a month and a half—no longer, I promise."

"It sounds interesting. Let's talk about it."

We walked to his office, where we met the director—Florian Rey, a famous Spanish filmmaker. "Greco! We've found you at last!"

"You certainly have."

As they told me what they had in mind, I began to concoct a plan of my own. Superficially, the film was nothing more than a nice adventure that paid reasonably well. But it was also an opportunity for me to audition the additional performers I needed for my company, costume them, and rehearse them into a state of high perfection—all without spending a nickel!

By the end of June 1948, we were all hard at work on the film. Including Nila, myself, Luis, and Carola, I had assembled a company of twenty-two dancers. I'd gotten them to sign up with me not only by telling them that we had a film to do, but also by telling them we had contracts to play in Paris, in Barcelona, in Madrid, and in a dozen other cities. I didn't have any contracts. Not one.

The filming dragged on and on, through June, through July, through August. During this time, I managed to arrange for just one booking: a two-week stint in an old Barcelona movie house. My people didn't know this, but they were getting restless nonetheless.

I talked to the producer. "Listen, I need a couple of weeks off. We're heading into the fall now. That's our season. I have to set up our tour. I have appointments all over Europe." I didn't have any, but I knew I'd better get some.

"Sure, go ahead. Just make sure you're back in two weeks, in case we have to do some more retakes."

"Of course."

Remembering the Spanish attaché's remarks about the Ballet Español, I had reason to hope Paris might be receptive to José Greco and Company. So without further ado, I grabbed my passport and caught the train for France.

I knew no Parisian impresarios or theater owners, but I did have one contact: my old friend, the Parisian correspondent for the *Christian Science Monitor*, an older man named Arno Dosch-Fleurot, the person who'd introduced me to Bob Kieve.

As soon as I got to Paris, Arno introduced me to all of that city's leading impresarios. The most important among them managed the Théâtre des Champs-Élysées, where Carmen Amaya had enjoyed a wonderful success only a few years earlier. I showed my credentials to this impresario—my photographs, my scrapbooks, my reviews.

"Jesus!" he said, impressed. "You could be another Carmen Amaya!"

"I hope so, yes."

"Tell me, Greco, can you open here, in my theater, in January?"

"January? No, as a matter of fact, my company and I have a date to fill in Barcelona."

"Well, then, how about February? Can you make it then?"

"February—of course."

"Excellent. Now listen, Greco, I'm going to schedule your group for one month. If you do well, we'll extend it. From there—if things work out—I'll see to it that you're booked throughout France: Bordeaux, Sete, Marseilles, Lyons, etc."

Now I had some breathing room.

I returned to Madrid with new confidence. We continued to work on *Manolete* well into September, doing retakes, shooting new scenes. I began to realize that the director, despite his fame, hadn't the least idea of what he was doing.

But I wasn't inclined to object. Through his largesse, I was keeping my company together, polishing our show, holding on until we opened in Barcelona in the first month of 1949.

One day, a strange lady showed up on the set. She waited patiently until I'd finished my work for the day, then came over and introduced herself.

"I'm Rajah Margo," she told me. "I'm the manager of Piereno Gamba" (now one of the world's greatest conductors).

"Piereno Gamba?"

"Yes—the famous child prodigy orchestra conductor."

"Ah, of course. What can I do for you?"

"Well, I've been hearing about this sensational Spanish dancer named Greco for a couple of years now. I'd like to talk to you about the possibility of your coming to Scandinavia. I'm the biggest impresario in that area."

We talked, over coffee. And, in a half hour, we'd reached complete agreement. After we finished our French tour, we'd go on to Malmö, Sweden, then Copenhagen, Denmark, then Oslo, Norway, and from there to Belgium. She would be my manager.

Suddenly, the future began to look promising.

Now all I had to worry about was the present. It was giving me plenty to be concerned about, too. *Manolete* had dragged on and on, through October, into November.

The original hundred thousand pesetas I'd been paid was now exhausted. So was the six thousand dollars I'd earned at the Barcelona night club. My little "family" and I were deep into our very meager savings.

Somehow we had to hold out until January. Somehow I had to get hold of enough cash to take my twenty-two-member company to Barcelona, then to Paris. But where? How?

I discussed my problem at length with Adrian Izquierdo, Pilar Lopez's manager and a good and knowledgeable friend. We came up with a unique idea: combining the operatic talents of my sister Norina with my dance talents, plus those of my company.

Izquierdo and I were so taken with this concept that we decided to risk everything—and I mean every last dime I had—on its success. We engaged a big theater in Madrid, hired the famous designer Capuletti to do the decor, and arranged for a forty-four-man symphony orchestra to play.

Izquierdo made it his business to publicize the event: "Adrian Izquierdo presents the eminent Metropolitan Opera singer, Norina

Greco, assisted by her brother, José Greco, the dancer." This message appeared on posters all over Madrid and on thousands of leaflets, each bearing the name of the theater and the date of our opening: November 20. I couldn't have asked for better publicity.

Three days before we were to open, the theater was completely sold out for the first performance. Izquierdo couldn't get over it. All he'd had to do to fill the theater was to announce the show.

Norina and I were also thrilled. Nothing would please us more than being able to work together. What a wonderful way it would be to solve Norina's career problems.

The theater was also half subscribed for the second night. Spanish audiences are usually cautious this way, though. They want to wait for word-of-mouth reports.

It all looked wonderful to me. If we played to good houses for a week or two, we'd have plenty of money for the upcoming tour.

We opened to a full house—and an expectant audience. The show began with a small aria by Norina, then Nila and one of the other dancers did a duet, then I did a little solo, then Norina came on to sing again.

Each part of the show drew a nice round of applause, but it became more and more obvious that the audience was waiting for the blockbuster. They were waiting to see me dance—*really* dance.

The truth was, they didn't give a damn about Norina or opera. They'd come to see José Greco. And they weren't getting enough of him. The production I'd devised wasn't what they wanted.

The reviews were polite enough, but it's word-of-mouth that sells theater tickets in Spain, not reviews. And the word-of-mouth was terrible. We'd joined a panther to a peacock and come up with one big yawn.

I remember the postmortems. We tried every rationalization—that we had enemies, that another opera singer was coming to town, that another dancer had just left, etc. Nonsense. We just misjudged the whole thing. It was a terrible combination.

We closed after the second night, having lost our entire investment. And there was no more where that had come from—not in my bank account. The question now was: How were we going to meet our tour obligations? How was I going to keep the company together?

It was obvious to Norina now that her career was pretty much at an end. And she felt it made no sense for her to stay with us in

Spain. She decided to return to Brazil, where she had many friends from her touring days.

Before she left, however, she wanted to give me some of her own savings, so we could meet our expenses, so our company could open in Barcelona and go on to Paris. The trouble was that her savings were all in Brazilian bank accounts. And Brazil and Spain weren't on speaking terms.

Norina wrote her closest friend in Brazil, however, and he promised that he'd get the money to Spain somehow. But the days dragged on. We began to economize on food. We cut back, even on necessities.

The time drew near for Norina to fly to Brazil—and still no money. We were now down to two meals a day.

"I don't understand it," Norina told us. "My friend in Brazil is extremely trustworthy. If he promises he's going to do something, he does it."

Day after day passed. No money. We were now truly desperate. "It's just not going to come, Norina," I said. "We'll have to find a loan somewhere, somehow. Maybe I'll sell the Fiat." It was my last possession of any value.

Finally, it was time to take Norina to the airport, to wish her farewell and Godspeed. What about the money? Well, something had gone wrong. Who could say what? I thought I might be able to borrow a little from Izquierdo.

We all went to the airport Nila, Luis, Norina, and I. Norina checked her luggage with the airline, went through immigration control, had her passport examined, etc.

Then we all sat down in the cafeteria. We ordered water, since we couldn't afford anything else. We were very near desperation.

"You know," Norina said, finally, breaking the silence, "why don't we call the apartment one last time and see if there's a message for me?"

"This late? At the last minute?"

"There's always a chance."

"All right, go ahead and call."

One of us had a coin for the telephone. Norina took it and disappeared. About five minutes later, she came running back, arms waving, an enormous smile on her face.

"Come on! Come on! Let's go back to Madrid. The money is there!"

That was only a slight exaggeration.

FIFTEEN

The money was coming into the country in Norina's name—therefore, only Norina could collect it. She had to present the telegram she'd been sent to a certain man in Madrid, a man with a very odd name. He would give her the money. Evidently, he did business in Brazil and could easily subtract from an account here and add to one there.

The problem was, was there time to go back to our apartment for the telegram, find this man in Madrid, get the money, and get back to the airport in time for Norina's plane? We checked with the airline. The plane had been delayed in Rome for two hours. We all leaped into the Fiat and sped off.

We stopped briefly at our apartment, picked up the telegram, then went looking for the address it mentioned. It was in an old part of town, far from the main section. The building itself was ancient and decrepit.

We went up the stairs, found the name on the door, and knocked. The door swung open and a man appeared in front of us. Past him, the room was almost totally dark. The only piece of furniture was a single chair.

"We're here to see so-and so," I said.

The man looked at us with raised eyebrows, appraising us. "Down the hall, turn left, go to the first door and knock."

He turned away from us and closed the door.

I exchanged glances with Norina. What was going on here? What kind of people were we dealing with? I was glad we'd come in a group.

We followed the first man's instructions and found the door he'd mentioned. Then we knocked. No response. We knocked again. No response. I put an ear to the door. There seemed to be no life inside.

Then, suddenly, I heard a hand at the knob. I leaped back as the door swung open, ever so slowly, squeaking ominously. Maybe they were just waiting for us to pick up the money so they could kill us and steal it.

"Yes?"

It was so dark, I could scarcely make out the man's features. But even in the dimness, his size did not escape me. He looked nearly seven feet tall. His expression was unremittingly grim.

"We have a telegram that instructs us to see Mr. so-and-so."

"Hmmn. Let me see it."

I handed him the telegram, certain that once it was out of my possession, all chance of getting the money was lost.

"Come in."

Doing our best to appear calm and confident, we entered the room. It contained a single wooden desk and two worn chairs.

"Who are all of these people?" the man asked Norina.

"My brother and his wife and her brother."

"Hmmn. Let me see your passport. And close the door."

Norina handed it to him. Next, I thought, he would ask for Nila's passport, then mine. That way, no one would be able to identify the bodies.

He sat down behind the desk, opened a drawer, and reached in. I was certain he was going to come up with a pistol. But no. He pulled out a stack of bills.

While we watched, he counted out the equivalent of two thousand dollars. Then he handed it to Norina. She thanked him politely—I could see her trembling—and we left as quickly as we could, without seeming to run.

Outside, there was jubilation. We'd done it! Everything would be all right now.

"Let's have a party!" Norina said.

"A party!" I said. "You've got to make a plane, remember? We'll go back to the airport and celebrate."

We made it with an hour to spare. Again, we entered the cafeteria. This time we ordered wine.

Now I was able to breathe again. Brother and sister had tried to help each other, and one of them, at least, had succeeded. We always seemed to be together when we needed each other most. And now we have those memories to share. Maybe that's one of the reasons we love each other so much.

The Ballets y Bailes de España de José Greco, as I called the company, opened in Barcelona, on January 12, on schedule. That was about the only good thing that happened there.

I didn't realize it, but I couldn't have picked a worse time. Those people who usually went to the theater had spent all of their money during the Christmas season.

For two weeks we played in Barcelona, we performed in front of audiences that rarely numbered 200. Usually, there were less than 150. Aside from the difficulties of putting on a show in these circumstances, I quickly found myself in financial trouble again. It cost me dearly every time we performed.

As if that weren't enough, the newspapers also gave me trouble. There were a few admiring reviews, but there was also some harsh criticism. Some journalist friends of Pilar Lopez castigated me in print for "having the audacity to present myself on stage" after abandoning the Ballet Español.

One newspaper interviewer even went so far as to humiliate me and make me sound like an idiot.

"Since you've been in Spain," he said, "have you found anything that has truly inspired you, anything connected to the dance?"

"As a matter of fact, yes. I am inspired by your gypsies. These artists may be unheralded, but they've given me many thrills."

"Well, if you had to see someone perform—at a party, for example—would you rather see the gypsies or would you rather see an established dancer such as Escudero?"

"Under those circumstances, I suppose I'd rather see the gypsies get up and do something spontaneously. But in a theater or on stage I would rather see Escudero. I put him on a pedestal."

The next day, my interview appeared in the newspaper under the headline, "Greco Prefers Gypsy Dancers over Escudero."

The day after that, the same newspaper carried an open letter to me from Escudero. "Italians should restrict themselves to singing opera and stay away from flamenco," he said.

A friendly newspaperman replied for me, in another open letter. "Señor Escudero would do well to remember that the greatest flamenco singer and dancer of all time was Silverio Franconetti, an Italian. Señor Greco follows in his footsteps."

Three days later, I got what I thought was a fan letter. I opened the envelope and found my friend's open letter clipped out of the paper and smeared with excrement. Evidently, Escudero was expressing his opinion of it to me.

Strangely enough, Escudero and I became good friends in later years, visiting each other, drinking together, and often discussing the old days. But we never mentioned what had happened between us that January in 1949.

Our flop in Barcelona—it was nothing less—forced me to borrow more money. Somehow, I had to get the company to Paris. There, I was sure, our fortunes would take a turn for the better.

Most of the dancers I'd hired were rather young and somewhat naïve. For the most part, they'd seen little of the world. Some of them had never been more than a few miles from their hometowns.

When our train pulled into Paris, then, they were astounded at the abundance they saw surrounding them. They couldn't get over the beautiful clothing, the expensive foods, the fine cars, and all the other signs of affluence that distinguished Paris in those days from, say, Madrid.

Several of them came to see me. "You're not paying us enough, Greco."

"You're getting the top dancers' salaries in Spain," I said.

"Yeah, but this is France. We want double the money you were paying or we won't perform."

"What do you mean you won't perform? We have a contract. You were admitted into this country as artists performing in my company."

"Screw the contract. Screw the government."

Who should be in town at that moment but Carmen Amaya. She was set to open a few days before I was. And what did my disgruntled artists do now but approach her and proclaim their availability.

Carmen Amaya took my guitarist away from me, hired my first dancers, even engaged my gypsy couple. My company was disappearing in front of my eyes. I would have come up with more money had I been able, but as it was I was in hock up to my eyebrows.

Somehow I managed to engage some third-rate performers to fill out my company. I rehearsed them frantically as opening night approached. Then, suddenly, I found myself with new troubles.

A delegate from the Society of Authors and Composers came to our rehearsal and watched us practice the number we did to Ravel's

"Bolero." The next day, we got a notice from Ravel's publishers that we could not use that piece, that it was the exclusive property of Pilar Lopez (when used to accompany a Spanish dance in Paris during that year).

No matter that I'd contracted with them two months earlier to use the piece, no matter that it was an integral part of our show, no matter that opening night was just a couple of days away. The "Bolero" was out.

Well, it wasn't. I had our musical director, Joaquina Marti, go through the entire score, note for note, and alter the melody—but nothing else. We wouldn't have to change a step—though the music might sound strange to the audience.

Now we were ready for Paris. The question was: Was Paris ready for us? At the time, the town was preoccupied with a man named Serge Lifar, the former director of the Paris Opera. Lifar had been fired because of allegations that he'd collaborated with the Germans.

But now World War II had been over for almost four years. The Pairs Opera re-engaged Lifar. He was going to appear there officially for the first time since his dismissal—on the very night we were due to open a few blocks away.

The newspapers were filled with nothing but what would happen when Lifar appeared. Demonstrations, riots, even bombs were freely predicted. Every Parisian interested in the theater—and certainly every newspaperman—was dying to find out what would happen.

The Paris Opera was mobbed that night. The Théâtre des Champs-Élysées—where we were—was nearly empty. But there were no demonstrations, riots, or bombs at the opera. Within twenty-four hours, Paris had forgotten Lifar.

Now our audiences began to grow. Newspaper reviewers drifted in to see us, one at a time, publishing their comments—most of which were highly favorable—not on the same day, but spread out. Incidentally, one reviewer said, "Greco's company did a truly stupendous dance to Ravel's 'Bolero.'"

Suddenly, people began to realize that the Ballets y Bailes de España de José Greco was something they shouldn't miss. Paris didn't exactly go crazy, as it had once over Carmen Amaya, but it responded to us with enthusiasm.

Our audiences grew larger and larger as the days passed. Soon I noticed that the very dancers who'd abandoned me for Carmen Amaya were coming to watch our show.

14. The great Argentinita. Her look and smile could light up an entire room.

15. Argentinita, myself, and Pilar Lopez, as we looked circa 1943 (PHOTO CREDIT: ALFREDO VALENTE).

16. Pilar Lopez and I, taken a few days after our opening in Madrid, in June 1946 (PHOTO BY HALSMAN).

17. Myself—with mustache —and Argentinita, in a humorous dance of the gay 1890s. This was taken in the early 1940s (PHOTO CREDIT: FRED FEHL).

18. Manolo Vargas, Argentinita, Pilar Lopez, and I
(PHOTO CREDIT: ALFREDO VALENTE).

19. Rehearsing for the film *Manolete*—while building my company.
I'm facing the camera.

20. Dancing with Nila. This picture
was taken in the late 1940s.

21. Nila.

22. Here I am as I was in Paris in 1948—so young, so young.

23. José Greco as I am.

24. October 1, 1951—my name, in lights, on Broadway. My mother loves this shot.

25. Jack Nonnenbacher. If you look closely, you, too, can see the humorous glint in his eye.

26. Dan Dailey, June Lockhart, and Jack Nonnenbacher, three of my favorite people (PHOTO CREDIT: IRVING L. ANTLER).

27. Myself, José Luis, and Nila, in a happy moment.

What they saw must have been quite educational: The audiences came, bought their tickets; watched the performance, and applauded vigorously. The dancers who'd defected simply weren't missed.

One by one, these dancers approached me—the same artists who'd quit when I was unable to double their salaries. They wanted back in, despite the troubles they'd caused me, despite the battles I'd had to fight with immigration on their behalf, despite the fact that the whole story had leaked out and damaged my reputation. And I took them back, most of them. Why, I don't really know. Perhaps it was a matter of loneliness.

A week after we opened, the Spanish attaché to France came backstage to visit us, to tell us how much he'd enjoyed the show.

"Believe it or not, I've seen it three times. And I like it better each time."

"I'm glad to hear it."

"You know, I have a very lovely friend who accompanied me this evening, an artist who did some sketches of you, Nila, and other members of your company while you performed. She'd love to meet you."

"Of course. Go get her and bring her back here, to my dressing room."

A few minutes later, the attaché returned with a beautiful woman —tall, with sparkling gray eyes and hair the color of champagne. She had a magnificent figure and extraordinarily sensual lips.

When she looked at me, I felt as if her total attention, her total being were focused on me. She devoured me with her eyes, not in any vulgar sense, but with flattering interest.

Her name was Laurie.

Many times, I have read that performers get great and lasting satisfaction from the applause and approval of their audiences. I always enjoyed this, of course. But it was never really enough for me.

Audiences are essentially anonymous. What I need, perhaps what any performer needs, is personal approbation. I want to know that I'm dancing for someone in particular and that this person is rejoicing in what I am doing.

The look that I received from Laurie that day—and so many times afterward—was the kind of reward I'd been hoping for. I felt I hadn't been dancing for some faceless mob, but for one special person.

A few days later, Laurie invited me—along with my entourage (Nila, Luis, and Joaquin)—to lunch at her studio, which was just a few blocks from the theater.

Laurie was not only a beautiful woman, she was brilliant and talented one, too. And before the lunch was over, we discovered that we had a great affinity for each other. I was drawn to her, to her femininity and charm.

It was at that lunch that she invited me to pose. This I did, a few days later. I went in hopes that I would find companionship. She did a beautiful portrait of me, which she wanted to give me. I refused, telling her to keep it, that it might be valuable someday.

"Well, in that case, would you come back and pose again? Now that I know you better, I think I can make an even better likeness."

So I went back and posed, several times. While I sat, Laurie and I talked, about art, about the dance, about life. She made me feel secure, and eased my loneliness. The initial affinity I'd felt turned into a compelling attraction.

We ended up loving.

In some ways, it was almost like being back with Phoebe again, my California love goddess. Laurie had passion and fervor and fire. But she had an elegance and class that surpassed even Phoebe.

My affair with Laurie went on throughout our two-month stay in Paris in 1949, and we renewed our relationship in 1950 and 1951. And I continued to see her in the early fifties, whenever I returned to Paris. On one occasion, I even met her in Spain—I wanted passionately to show her the Spain I loved, to share with her its splendor, its explosive beauty.

My relationship with Laurie had an important impact on my performances, I'm sure. While I was seeing her, I felt as though I was the most exciting, most potent individual in the world—that's how she made me feel. I felt as though I were exuberantly partaking of the best of what life had to offer. And I performed accordingly. She'd given me new self-confidence.

And where was Nila, my wife, when all this was going on? She was there in Paris, with me, suspecting not a thing. I never once stinted on my obligations toward her, nor did my affection for her waver.

Something had changed between us, however. It was subtle, but it was real. Nila's dependency, Nila's illnesses, Nila's need for me had changed my feelings toward her. More and more, I felt myself her big brother.

From time to time, of course, I felt guilty about what I was doing. After all, Nila had been—and was—a good wife. As marvelous as Laurie was, Nila was also wonderful. She did not suffer by comparison. But ours was not a relationship of equals.

We played in Paris for two months, until the end of March 1949. By that time I'd managed to convince my Parisian impresario that I could do well elsewhere in France, too.

The South of France, particularly, was filled with Spanish immigrants and Spanish workers, who had come to live there or to work the mines and the fields in the area. They longed to partake of Spanish culture. José Greco and his company of Spanish dancers would be a natural there.

And so we spent the spring touring—in Bordeaux, Toulouse, Arles, Marseilles, Toulon, Cannes, and Nice. It was a profitable tour. We earned enough that I could pay back all the money I'd borrowed in Spain.

But it was not without its troubles.

We were traveling by bus that spring—chartered Pullman bus, the kind where most of the luggage is carried on top.

One night, after performing in Perpignan, a city near France's border with Spain, almost on the Mediterranean, we had dinner, then got on our bus. We were to perform in Marseilles the next afternoon, and we hoped to get some sleep as we drove there, during the night. It was a five-hour trip.

I remember going to the back of the bus, where we carried our curtains, curling up in them, and quickly dozing off. (In those days, we had to carry our curtains with us, since few theaters provided their own.)

About an hour out of Perpignan, traveling along the coastal highway, we ran into a tremendous rainstorm. Something woke me up— evidently the rain beating on the bus roof. It was pitch black outside —no moon, no stars, no lights in view.

Then I heard another noise, an odd thumping. I thought something must be wrong with one of the tires. Maybe we'd had a flat. It wasn't so far from here that I'd had a number of flats myself, in my little Fiat.

I saw Joaquin sitting just in front of me. "Joaquin," I said, "would you mind going forward and telling the driver that there's something wrong with one of the rear tires? Maybe we have a flat."

He nodded and started up the aisle. At that moment, we went through a small village, and a few lights from the houses momentarily illuminated the road.

"Aaiie! Look at that!" One of the dancers screamed, pointing out the window.

I looked up just in time to see a suitcase fly by. What was this?

The driver pulled off the road and we piled out of the bus to see what was happening. Half of the company's suitcases were gone. They'd fallen off the bus somewhere along the road.

Well, imagine the screams of my performers. They wanted to kill me or kill the driver, or commit some sort of mayhem to express their anger.

Of course, we turned around and went back, but we could find only two or three of the suitcases. It may be that some cars following us picked up the rest and made off with them.

For some of my artists, this was a disaster of the first order. Everything they had was in those suitcases—their clothing, their money, their valuables. They stood there in the rain, crying.

We brought the remaining suitcases inside the bus, took our seats again, and started off, thankful that we hadn't lost everything.

The bus didn't pull into Marseilles until about 4:00 A.M. And when it did, we all headed for the hotel—and bed. Fortunately, Nila's and my suitcases weren't among those lost. We each took one into the hotel with us.

At about eight the next morning, our company manager, Diego de Diego (husband of our pianist, Joaquina Marti) came knocking at my door.

"José, José, come quickly! Someone has broken into our bus!"

I was still half asleep, but I dressed quickly and went down to the plaza in front of the hotel, where the bus had been parked. I was worried about the luggage, but I was even more worried about our costumes.

As it turned out, thieves had taken every single suitcase. But they hadn't touched the costumes, which were in those huge theatrical trunks (the very same ones I'd taken to Montorio). I guess the trunks were too big for them.

But every company member's personal baggage—mine included—was gone, except for what we'd taken into the hotel with us that night. It was nothing short of a catastrophe.

We appealed to the bus company, which ended up giving each

person ten or fifteen dollars—not much if someone has lost all his savings or all of his good clothing.

To try to bolster morale—it had sunk to a new low—I took everyone out to dinner for a week and I raised everyone's salary as much as I could. But some began to feel that the Greco company was jinxed. Even in the midst of success, catastrophe found us.

I admit to having my own doubts. It was now the end of May 1949, almost exactly a year since I'd left Pilar Lopez. And it had been nothing more than one struggle after another. Was this the way it was always going to be?

We returned to Paris, our tails between our legs. Even Laurie couldn't cheer me up. Then we boarded a train headed for Scandinavia, to continue our tour, this time under the auspices of Rajah Margo.

I was deeply concerned about what lay ahead of us. The Scandinavians had a reputation for being cold and hard to impress. I worried that they'd take one look at my exuberant, gaily dressed Spanish dancers and dismiss our show as a frivolity they could easily do without.

As I sat in my compartment, looking out at the passing landscape, my thoughts were a mixture of conflicting emotions. On one hand, I had premonitions of doom, a fear that my success might not continue in the years to come. On the other, I had self-confidence, born of the strong preparation I'd undergone and the strong base I'd built for myself.

I suppose I imagined every possible result of our Scandinavian tour—except, of course, the one that actually came to pass.

SIXTEEN

My company and I weren't the only ones concerned about how we'd be received in Scandinavia. Rajah Margo was also on pins and needles. She'd arranged for us to appear all over Scandinavia and northern Europe. Any setback we suffered would be her setback too.

Before we played in Copenhagen—the big time—Rajah wanted us to perform out of town, so we could get used to Scandinavian audiences and they to us, so that some favorable publicity—we hoped—could be generated, and Copenhagen's appetite for us whetted.

The city she chose for this initial engagement was Malmö, a Swedish town of about two hundred thousand people, on the Öresund—the Sound—fifteen miles from Copenhagen, a short boat trip.

We arrived in Malmö early in June, for a four-day appearance at the fantastic new Staatstheater there. Normally, we would have been scheduled for at least a couple of weeks in such a city, but the theater held six thousand people. We'd have to be lucky to fill it.

Rajah Margo had done her work well. When curtain time came, on that first night in Malmö, the theater was full. It was all up to us now, and the unpredictable chemistry between performers and audiences.

Five minutes after the show began, we knew the result. For reasons we could not comprehend, the Swedes, known the world over for their self-control and emotional reserve, went wild.

We simply couldn't do anything wrong. More than that, we couldn't do anything that didn't produce an incredible response in the audience. Those calm, self-contained Swedes applauded until their palms were red, and they cheered until their voices were little more than croaks.

When the curtain fell, we rushed into each other's arms and hugged and kissed. It was as if we had passed our most demanding test. The fears and doubts we'd taken with us from France vanished like so much cigarette smoke.

As we were congratulating ourselves, a lady came backstage to show me that she'd broken her wedding ring in two because she'd applauded me so vigorously. She was happy the stone—a large diamond—hadn't been lost, but she seemed even more happy to meet the company face-to-face.

Then I heard that another lady—who'd been more than eight months pregnant—got so excited with what was happening on stage that she'd had to be taken out of the orchestra. While she was recovering in the lobby, she gave birth to a healthy baby girl!

That night, we celebrated—our company joined, on this occasion, by Rajah Margo; by Kristen Södring, the Danish impresario who was to present us in Copenhagen; and by Svend Krah Jacobsen, a writer for the Berlinske Tidende, Copenhagen's most prestigious newspaper. He'd seen our show in Paris, loved it, and become friendly with us.

The next day, we were the toast of Malmö. Some of that town's most eminent citizens showed us the city, its beautiful parks and museums. We were invited to parties after our performances for the balance of our stay.

Best of all was the enthusiasm of Kristen Södring, who'd come to Malmö with grave doubts that we could be a success in his theater in Copenhagen.

"Of course, I can't be certain, José, but my experience has been that any act that does well in Malmö is a sensation in Copenhagen. The Danes are very warm, open-hearted people, you know."

At the time, I would have been more than happy to settle for a reception like the one we'd gotten in Malmö. After all, we'd filled that enormous theater four days running—twenty-four thousand people had seen us. But if I had settled for success on that order, I would have been cheating myself.

We left Malmö much buoyed by our reception there. But Copenhagen was no small hick town. It was the Paris of Scandinavia, one of the two or three most sophisticated cities in all of Europe. Södring was sure we'd do well there, but I knew only time would tell.

We were booked for a three-week run in Copenhagen, into a tiny, jewel-like theater that seated less than one thousand people. It was an absolutely perfect place for our show. For one thing, our drops and decors fit the scale of the theater—they hadn't in Malmö. For another, the theater's small size would tend to magnify the impact of our performance.

Opening night in Copenhagen was one of the most incredible experiences in my life. Seville had been exceptional, Malmö gratifying, but Copenhagen was not to be believed.

Throughout our performance, the audience response had been little short of deafening. Each number had produced such applause that the entire show had stretched out fifteen minutes beyond its normal length.

But we didn't truly realize how we had impressed the Danes until the curtain fell. They quite literally went out of their minds. They wouldn't stop applauding! They began to rip the theater apart—and believe me, I'm not exaggerating.

We went out and did bows and encores, encores and bows, bows and encores—it looked as though the show wouldn't be over until the next night's audience was in the lobby, waiting to take their seats.

Finally, the theater management had to call the police! Only after the gendarmes arrived was order restored. Only after the police had made a show of force did the patrons reluctantly get up from their seats and file out of the theater.

Backstage, we looked at each other in wonderment. What kind of a monster had we unleashed here? Was this the way it was going to be every night, after every performance?

The answer turned out to be "Yes."

Something happened in Copenhagen in June of 1949 that I still cannot explain. We touched some buried nerve in the Danes. We triggered some kind of explosive release unlike anything I'd ever seen or heard of.

Why did this happen in Copenhagen and not in Barcelona or Paris or Madrid? Who knows? Perhaps the very reserve of the Scandinavians worked in our favor. Perhaps we provided the catalyst they needed in order to achieve a release.

Perhaps it took a people like the Spaniards, with their music and their sunshine and their dancing and their guitars and their flaring skirts and mantillas to break through the Danes' self-imposed austerity, to erase the grim memories of war.

This fantastic response to me and to my company—but especially to me—was not limited to the theater. The newspapers were filled, day after day, not simply with criticism (all of it laudatory), but also with features. It seemed that all anyone in Copenhagen could talk about was Greco.

"Have you seen Greco yet?"

"Isn't Greco great?"

"I'd pay anything for a ticket to see Greco."

"Greco is the biggest thing that ever happened to Copenhagen."

God help me, in that summer, anyhow, I was. I was more loved than Hans Christian Andersen, more admired than the Little Mermaid, more celebrated than the combined output of all the pastry shops in Denmark. I was—or at least they called me—the "Toledo Blade."

Copenhagen had come down with a virus the newspapers dubbed "Greco Fever," a disease from which it did not quickly recover. The same thing had happened to Frank Sinatra, in America, a few years earlier, and it would happen again when Elvis Presley became popular, and once more when the Beatles appeared.

Not only was this an artistic triumph, it was also a personal triumph of a magnitude I'd never conceived possible. I think I met—and was befriended by—every important person in Copenhagen that summer. I dined in the homes of the rich and famous, partied with the important and influential.

I scarcely had time to reflect on the incongruity of it all. Here I was, an Italian kid from Brooklyn who'd become a Spanish dancer and, by some quirk of fate, had become the toast of Scandinavia. No novelist would have dared suggest such a plot.

So remarkable was my reception in this normally cold northern city that it sent shock waves throughout the world. Correspondents from Italy, Mexico, France, Spain, Boston, Switzerland, Los Angeles, and a dozen other places wrote accounts for their newspapers about this remarkable Danish mania.

While I was performing in Copenhagen, a strange (but natural) event occurred that almost seemed intended to honor me. The sun refused to set. It lit the sky for more than forty-eight hours straight. This was, of course, the famous midnight sun, an annual occurrence in northern lands. This year, it seemed to be shining for me.

Some of the adulation that came my way was, not surprisingly, quite personal. There was a lovely young Swedish girl named Toby, a dancer who was also represented by Rajah Margo. Toby was caught in a disastrous marriage, and she sought comfort in my arms. I did my best to help her.

Then there was Yvonne, a lovely and talented lady, an artist who was fascinated by me and my dancing. We also had a brief liaison. It was not so much physical as emotional and intellectual.

Did I feel guilty about seeing these women? Not really. An artist —especially such a celebrated artist as I—is entitled to his little peccadillos, isn't he? That's what these were, peccadillos, passing relationships that offered no real threat to my life with Nila. Laurie, of course, was something else. But she was also someplace else at the time.

Besides, I was riding the crest. There were adulation, praise, and affection wherever I turned—recognition I not only enjoyed but also needed. How could I have refused tribute from these lovely ladies? Why should I have refused?

There was also money, of course—not really in proportion to the magnitude of our success (I'm not sure there was enough money in all of Denmark for that), but enough for me to pay my artists, pay off my loans, and even put a little money in the bank.

Suddenly, we came to the last performance in our run. The three weeks had gone by in an instant. This last performance was just as remarkable as the first.

Of course, the audience went wild each time we finished a number. It didn't matter what we did—a *farucca*, a *siguiriya*, a *soleares*, a *jota*, whatever. But it was after the curtain fell that the real craziness began anew.

There were bows and encores, encores and bows—and still the audience kept up the applause, all together, in rhythm. They were having so much fun that we also decided to have some fun.

I'd take a bow, then I'd go offstage and another member of the company would take a bow. Then I'd reappear—minus part of my costume. Then another member of the company would come on, in my place. Then I'd reappear, this time partly dressed in street clothing.

This went on and on, until every member of the company had changed from his costume into street clothing—and still they applauded. In all, this lasted for 40 minutes. Someone counted up 180 separate curtain calls. Insanity, glorious insanity.

We now had two months free before we were to continue our tour. Holland, Belgium, Luxemburg, and Switzerland awaited us when the summer was over. Most of the company went back to Spain.

In Madrid, I paid off a year's accumulation of debts, then went on to Barcelona and did the same thing there. I was forever paying off debts. I still am. But then, aren't we all?

While I was in Spain, another dance company—a group from the Caribbean—arrived in Copenhagen and opened at the theater we'd left only a week earlier.

Ten days after I'd departed from Copenhagen, I got a call from Rajah Margo. The Caribbean dance company had flopped. "Could you come back and play another three weeks, José?"

"Now?"

"Now."

Well, we went back. And it was as if we'd never left. Södring again filled the theater to the rafters for three weeks running, even though he'd raised the prices. The audiences acted exactly as they had before. If I'd run for mayor of Copenhagen that summer, my opponent wouldn't have gotten a vote.

Of course, we hadn't succeeded in such a magnificent fashion anywhere else. In Copenhagen, José Greco was a star of the first magnitude, and the José Greco dance company was the hottest attraction in years. But what about elsewhere? That remained to be seen.

"Are you interested in doing the rest of Scandinavia this summer?" Rajah Margo asked me. "After the Copenhagen publicity, I can book you anywhere. It would keep you busy until you started to tour the Low Countries this fall."

"Why not?"

We swept through Scandinavia, audiences greeting us with the same sort of fervor they'd shown in Copenhagen. We went back to Malmö and to several other Swedish cities—Göteborg, Norrkoping, and Stockholm.

Then we played in Denmark's other major cities—Aarhus and Odense. From there, we went to Norway—to Bergen, Stavanger, and Oslo.

In Oslo, Nila and I were in the lobby of our hotel when we noticed two American couples looking at a poster—the very poster that was announcing our appearance. They were planning their evening.

"Nila, isn't that Fredric March?"

"My God, it is."

I walked up to the man.

"Excuse, me, you're Fredric March, aren't you?"

"Why, yes, I am."

"Well, pardon me for eavesdropping, but I'm José Greco—the man you're going to see tonight. I'd very much appreciate it if you'd be my guests."

"How wonderful, José. We'd love to."

And he introduced us to his wife, Florence Eldridge, and his associate, George Macy, the Random House executive, and his daughter, who was a ballet dancer. Thus began a friendship that was to last for years.

You'd think, I suppose, that my money troubles were mostly over by this time. Well, they weren't. They aren't, even now. Maybe they never will be. But it wasn't a matter of not having enough. My problem, in those days, was that I wasn't getting paid the right *kind* of money.

I was being paid in Danish *kroner*, Norwegian *kroner*, and Swedish *kronor*. At the time, these currencies were not easily convertible into dollars or pounds or other readily acceptable currencies. Money earned in these countries had to be spent in these countries; only a small part of it could be exchanged.

Unfortunately, I couldn't get enough dollars to pay the company's travel costs, the salaries, and the other expenses. I was constantly borrowing and begging.

One day, Joaquin, who hated to see me struggle with such problems, came to me with an idea.

"José, let me take our money to Switzerland. It's a free market. Any currency can be changed into any other currency there. I'll go with *kroner* or *kronor* and come back with dollars."

"I'm desperate, Joaquin. Let's try it, maybe it will work."

I knew I could count on Joaquin. There was no one else in the world who was so loyal, so trustworthy, so willing to help. I took him to the airport.

What an odd figure he made, in his funny black hat, his thick brown overcoat, carrying an enormous leather satchel stuffed with money. He was like a character out of *Alice in Wonderland*.

This was the first of I don't know how many trips—as many as a dozen a year. Joaquin became a familiar figure in Switzerland and on European airlines of every nationality. I wonder what people made of him.

That winter, after touring the Low Countries, Nila and I headed back to New York, by boat. We were going home for the holidays. I was a big star; I could afford to splurge now.

I felt as though I had the world in the palm of my hand, as if all my troubles were over. The truth was, all my real troubles were ahead of me. But, for that matter, so were my real successes.

SEVENTEEN

By the end of January, our little entourage—Nila and I, her brother Luis, Carola Goya, and Joaquin were back together again in Madrid. Our 1950 season was to begin in the middle of March, so I immediately started rounding up the rest of the company.

At the end of the previous season I'd let our company manager—Diego de Diego—go. He was a very likable man, but he wasn't suited to the job. Soon after, his wife, Joaquina Marti—our pianist and musical director—told me that she would not be rejoining us in 1950. Her first loyalty was to her husband. I understood.

Now I found that she'd done more than simply quit. She'd taken fully half my company—twelve dancers—and formed a company of her own. Furthermore, by undercutting my fee, she'd managed to get a number of bookings.

I wasn't really worried about the competition. She might have had my dancers, but she didn't have my name—which, in the last year especially, had come to mean a great deal. My problem was replacing her and the many artists she'd taken with her.

Bit by bit, I began to fill out my company, picking up dancers here and there throughout Spain, dancers who'd worked with one company or another but weren't presently employed.

Among these was an attractive girl named Lola de Ronda, whom I'd known when we were both with the Pilar Lopez company. She was an excellent dancer and her appearance added a lot to my company, but if I'd known of the trouble she was going to cause me in the future, I doubt that I would have taken her on.

My biggest problem was replacing Joaquina Marti. In a dance company such as mine, the pianist is vital. She—or he—must have a broad repertoire, be able to play under a wide variety of conditions, and be able to adjust to sometimes unexpected changes on stage.

I'd managed to hire a young American pianist, at least for the beginning of the tour, but I knew he wouldn't last for long. He had many other interests. He wanted to be a soloist, or to accompany opera singers.

In the early part of February, Rajah Margo and I went to Paris to find someone who would take on the job permanently. The man we were hoping to engage was Roger Machado, who had accompanied Argentinita long before I'd danced with her and who had since become one of Europe's most eminent pianists.

Machado and I had an almost immediate meeting of the minds. I'd seen him with Argentinita and respected him enormously. He'd seen me in Paris and had loved my work. Within an hour after we'd met, we'd drawn up a mutually agreeable contract.

Machado arranged to meet the company on May 1, in Amsterdam, after we'd spent six weeks touring Switzerland, France, and Belgium. He'd agreed to be with us for at least the rest of the year. As it turned out, Machado—Maestro, we called him—was with us year after year, with a few short interruptions, for twenty-five years!

And so we started our tour.

One worry that Nila and I had during this period concerned her brother Luis Olivares, a slender, good-looking fellow in his early twenties. For reasons we couldn't understand, he'd taken an interest in Carola Goya, a classic dancer who was in her late fifties.

Nila and I felt it was not a healthy relationship. Under Carola's influence, Luis was kind of drying up, aging in front of our eyes, almost unnaturally.

Fortunately—or so we thought—the answer to the problem was at hand: Lola de Ronda, the girl I'd just hired. From my previous association with her, I knew her friends and family, as did Nila. Lola felt at home with us and we felt comfortable with her. She was a nice girl, an innocent girl.

Every chance we got, Nila and I arranged to throw Luis and Lola together, in hopes that some spark would catch, that she'd lure him away from Carola. And sure enough, that is exactly what happened. But how little do we anticipate the consequence of our good deeds.

On May 1, we arrived in Amsterdam. Machado was there to meet us.

"When do we rehearse?" he asked, by way of greeting.

"Well, right now, if you want."

"Let me see the music."

Machado was never reluctant to get down to work. We found a piano in the hotel, and Machado sat down to play. It was as if he'd been with me for years. He was perfect. The next day, he rehearsed with the company. One run-through was quite enough.

That night, when the moment for the performance came, the Maestro appeared in absolutely classical attire—a tuxedo complete with tails. He had such bearing, such dignity, such naturalness that I said to myself, "that's exactly right—no Spanish costumes for the Maestro."

The effect on stage was stunning. When the curtains opened and Machado took his place at the piano, the audience broke into spontaneous applause. He hadn't done a thing, and there was nothing and nobody else on stage—and already there was applause. I began to realize how fortunate I'd been to find the Maestro.

That year, we played the big summer resorts in the Low Countries—Ostend, Scheveningen, The Hague, etc. Each had huge, splashy theaters with adjacent casinos—like Las Vegas or Monte Carlo. The theaters drew the crowds, and the casinos made the whole thing pay off.

Then we went back to Scandinavia for an even more lucrative tour than the first one. I was welcomed back to the same theaters, in the same cities, and was treated the same way. It was almost as if I were returning home.

During this tour, I renewed my acquaintance with Yvonne. And, of course, there were idyllic interludes in Paris with Laurie. I had little reason to complain about what life had to offer.

What I really wanted, however, was not a series of romantic liaisons, but a home and a family—some stability in my life. I wanted to settle down with Nila and create a place to which I could return after each tour.

Toward the end of 1950, she and I visited the Italian Riviera. There we found a beautiful spot, near an elegant little community called Forte dei Marmi (Fortress of Marble), so named because it served as the port city for Carrara, the great marble center. There we bought a homesite and engaged an architect.

Soon after this I was approached by an impresario who wanted our company to play in Argentina. He'd seen Roland Petit's *Carmen* in

New York, where it had been a sensation, and he wanted to imitate both the show and its success in South America, only with a Spanish flavor.

His plan was to divide our performance into two parts. In the first, the company would do its usual numbers. The entire second half, however, would be devoted to *Carmen*, which he would direct.

All of our artists, myself included, would take part in both halves of the program, except that Nila would be replaced in the second part by a famous South American dancer, who would play the title role, Carmen, the role created in New York by Zizi Jeanmaire.

Nila wasn't very enthusiastic about this arrangement, of course, but since we had nothing going on between March 1 and June 1 (when we were to open in London, at the Sadler's Wells Theatre), I agreed. The contract—the money—was excellent. Besides, the tour would give me a chance to spend some time with my sister Norina.

And so, when we finished our European tour, the company packed up and boarded a boat for South America. It was not a pleasant trip. Nila got sick almost immediately, worse than ever before. She suffered from excruciating stomach pains, pains so terrible that she had to spend the entire trip under sedation.

At São Paulo, Brazil, we visited with Norina. I told her of my plans to make myself a home in Forte dei Marmi, in Italy, and she was so delighted that she contributed five thousand dollars of her own money to get the construction started.

We arrived in Buenos Aires a few days before we were due to open. Nila was still sick—so sick, in fact, that she had to be carried off the boat. Performing with the company was out of the question for her.

We might have been a spectacular success in Argentina, but that country happened to be in the midst of a problem so typical of the area—political unrest.

There was trouble with Eva Peron, trouble with the unions, trouble with the syndicates. The whole country was in turmoil. And there we were, a Spanish dance company, hoping to draw an audience.

Looking back, it was a miracle that we opened at all, because of the strikes. The stagehands didn't finish hanging the decors, they didn't finish getting the theater ready, but somehow we managed.

We played in Buenos Aires for several weeks, to sizable audiences.

Despite the political unrest, we did reasonably well. The impresario promised to send us a check for our share of the proceeds—approximately ten thousand dollars.

He arranged for the company to return to Barcelona, by boat, but because of Nila's health, I decided that she and I should fly back. At the airport, we ran into unanticipated trouble.

"I'm sorry, Señor Greco," a customs official told me, "but you can't leave the country until you declare your income and pay your taxes."

"Income? But I haven't been paid yet."

"Yes, but according to your impresario's declaration, you made two hundred thousand pesos."

"Maybe he owes me that much, but I haven't seen it yet."

"That doesn't matter, Señor Greco. You will have to pay your taxes on that amount, or we will be forced to detain you."

In the end, the Argentine Government took everything I had—all my cash, all my traveler's checks. They even took the money I was going to use to buy our airline tickets! We were being mugged by the government.

I called Norina. "Listen, I'm in a little jam. . . ."

She sent me money for the plane tickets.

As we boarded our plane, we looked back at beautiful Buenos Aires—for the last time. I had no intention of returning. We felt we'd been lucky to escape this madhouse with the clothing on our backs.

As usual, we'd stayed too long. The only way to get to London in time to meet our obligations there was to fly to Natal, in northern Brazil (where the distance between South America and Africa is shortest), then to Casablanca, then to Spain, then to London.

We arrived in Natal at dusk and transferred to KLM for the eight-hour flight to Casablanca. Nila and I settled down in our seats, hoping to get some sleep. I took a window seat, just behind the wing.

For some reason, I couldn't sleep—though everyone else in the plane dozed off quickly. I gazed out the window at the stars. Suddenly I saw a little light on one of the engines. It took me a few seconds to realize that the engine was on fire.

I looked around the cabin, but not another soul was awake. Nila was sleeping peacefully beside me, her stomach trouble somewhat better, thank God. I looked out the window again. To my horror, the engine was now completely ablaze! I felt the fear rising in me.

As I stared, the entire engine was engulfed in flames, flames bright enough to light up the sky. Yet inside the plane, all was peaceful. I didn't know what to do. Surely the pilot knew of the trouble, and yet . . .

Suddenly, the engine fell off!

The plane dipped slightly, then leveled out again. Beside me, Nila stirred.

"We're going through some rough weather," I told her. "Why don't you take off your shoes and relax?"

"What? Why? I'm half asleep."

"Fine. Then continue to sleep."

We landed just south of Casablanca, without further incident—to my great relief. But we were delayed there for most of the next day, because of "equipment trouble." No further explanation was offered. And no one inquired. I was the only passenger who knew what had happened.

When we arrived in Spain, we found that the rest of the company had been forced to travel steerage—not the promised tourist class. It seemed that the impresario had traded in the tickets and pocketed the difference.

As for the ten thousand dollars he owed us, we never saw it.

EIGHTEEN

Now we went to England, to begin our engagement at the prestigious Sadler's Wells Theatre, as part of the Festival of Great Britain. It was an extraordinary honor for our company, not only to be a part of the festival, but also to play at Sadler's Wells.

Sadler's Wells—a name synonymous with Nijinsky and Diaghilev —was now operating under the auspices of Covent Garden, London's equivalent to Carnegie Hall, the entire operation being sponsored by the government.

Until we performed there, that theater had been reserved for the top concert artists of the day—the most eminent violinists, pianists, and singers in the world. We were the first company of Spanish dancers ever to appear there.

We opened to the kind of reception I'd come to expect—thunderous applause and full houses—and began our month's run at the theater. We were scheduled to spend the rest of the summer touring Scandinavia—for the third time. After that, who knew? The plans had yet to be made.

Little did I know it then, but my future, my plans not only for the rest of 1951, but also for the rest of my life, were being determined at that moment in a dingy little movie house on the French Riviera.

That theater happened to be showing *Manolete*, the film my company and I had made in Spain in 1949. And in the audience, quite by chance, was a man named Lee Shubert, the famous American theater owner.

By this time, I'd pretty much forgotten about *Manolete*. It had been a financial disaster, contributing not a penny more than the original fee I'd been paid.

About the only thing of interest concerning the film had been the reception afforded the dance numbers. Time after time, after the numbers were shown, audiences had demanded that the film be stopped, rewound, and the dance numbers shown again.

At any rate, I'd just finished a performance at Sadler's Wells and was in my dressing room, changing into street clothing, when there was a knock on the door.

"Yes."

"Excuse me, Mr. Greco. I am Albert de Courville. Could I speak to you for a moment?"

"Come in."

A tall, elderly gentleman opened my door and entered.

"Who did you say you were?"

"Albert de Courville. I am the representative of Lee Shubert."

"Lee Shubert? The Lee Shubert of the Shubert theaters, in America?"

"That's right."

"The Lee Shubert who owns the Shubert Theater on Forty-fourth Street, near Broadway, in New York?" How well I knew the place, from my days as a ticket runner. The Atlas Agency had been only a few doors down the street.

"The same."

"Well, what can I do for you?"

"Mr. Shubert saw you in a movie when he was in Cannes a few days ago. I believe it was called *Manolete*. He asked me to find out if you could come to the United States. He wants you to open at the Shubert Theater in New York on October 1. After that, he plans to offer you a six-month contract to perform in America."

"What's your name again?"

I called Rajah Margo in Copenhagen. She was sick, terminally ill, as it turned out, and unable to come to London to advise me. But she told me how much to ask for, what conditions to demand, etc.

I was in the midst of considering how to respond to Lee Shubert when I got a telephone call from Sol Hurok. Suddenly the world was beating a path to my door.

"How have you been, José?"

"Fine, Pop. And you?"

"Very good. Hey, I understand you've been talking to Lee Shubert."

"You certainly are good at finding things out, Pop. Yes, you're right. He's offering me a six-month contract."

"Are you going to bring the whole company?"

"Why do you ask?"

"Tell you what, José—can you come to Paris so we can talk?"

The next weekend, I met Hurok at the Hôtel Meurice, where he was staying. We talked over lunch.

"Times have certainly changed, haven't they, José?"

"Certainly have, Pop."

"How long ago was it when the Marquis de Cuevas and I were getting you out of that little jam in Chicago?"

"Oh, yes, that. About six years, I suppose."

"Well, we don't have to dwell on the old days, do we?"

"Of course not. All of that is past."

"Good. Now, José, I want you to come under my auspices. It would be 'S. Hurok presents José Greco.' Think of it, wouldn't it be wonderful? I'd love it."

"That's great, Pop. But I have a company of twenty people."

"Forget them, José. You don't need them. All you need is a couple of girl dancers, another male dancer, perhaps, and a guitarist-pianist. It will be just like Argentinita or Escudero."

"I don't know. . . ."

"Come on, José, I'll give you a contract—four years at three thousand dollars a week. What do you say?"

I took a deep breath. "Pop, you are right when you said the times have changed. Audiences aren't satisfied with that sort of thing anymore. They want a spectacle, not an intimate revue. They want all the flair and verve that an entire company can provide."

"You're telling me what audiences want?"

"Listen, Pop, I respect your knowledge. You know that. But I'm not interested in recitals or night clubs or concert dates. I'm not interested in being another Escudero or in imitating Argentinita. I want to make the Spanish dance a *theater* attraction."

"Can't be done, José. From my experience, I know. . . ."

"But from my experience, I know it can. I've seen it, in Paris, in Copenhagen, in Amsterdam, in London—I've seen it everywhere in Europe."

"But we're talking about America now, José."

"Are people so different in America?"

Hurok shrugged.

"Pop, I'll tell you what. Shubert is offering me six thousand dollars a week plus transportation. If you're willing to match that, I'll sign with you. But it's my whole company or nothing."

Hurok took a sip of wine, then wiped his lips and smiled. "I think you're making a mistake, José. But best of luck, anyhow."

Two days later, while I was performing in London, Albert de Courville showed up again with a contract.

"No," I said, "I'm not signing—not until you see the show."

"I don't have to see the show, Mr. Greco. My employer simply wants me to get your signature."

"I don't care what he wants. I just can't sign until you've seen me and you've approved my show." I needed the recognition, I needed the personal contact.

A few weeks later, de Courville came to see us while we were performing at Ostend, Belgium. After the show, he came backstage.

"That was unbelievable, Mr. Greco. Finest thing I've ever seen, by far."

"Thank you, Mr. de Courville."

"Will you sign now?"

"Yes, of course."

And I put my name to the contract. With a stroke of the pen, I'd gained entry to all the Shubert theaters in America, from Bangor, Maine, to Miami Beach, from New York to Seattle, from Seattle to San Diego.

Did de Courville mean what he'd said? I don't know. But I needed to have him say it.

My company and I continued our tour, traveling now to Copenhagen. When I got there, I was met by a Shubert representative, who said his job was to handle publicity and make travel arrangements. "Go ahead," I said, "do your job."

He began taking pictures of me and the rest of my company; then he went to work on getting us all plane tickets for our return to the United States.

It was late August now, about six weeks until we were to open in New York. Finally I had a chance to write my mother and tell her all that had happened.

But that very night, when I returned from my hotel after a performance, I found a wire waiting for me. It was from Mama. "Dear Costanzo," she said, "the strangest thing has happened. Someone has taken your picture and put it up on billboards all over Broadway. What does this mean? What's going on?"

For a moment, I was as puzzled as she had been. Then I realized that the mighty Shubert organization had gone into high gear. My picture on Broadway! Who could have believed it?

I placed a transatlantic call to Mama and explained.

"Costanzo," she told me, "you've made me feel twenty-five years younger."

For the next six weeks, Mama barraged me with letters, sending me photographs of the pictures outside the Shubert Theater, clippings of the newspaper ads, and news of how well the tickets were selling.

Each day, she'd call the Shubert Theater.

"Hello," she'd say, "I'd like to reserve some seats for the José Greco show."

"I'm sorry, ma'am, we're sold out."

Then the next day she'd call again.

"Could I order two seats for the José Greco show?"

"We're sold out until November, lady."

And she'd call again.

"I want ten seats to the José Greco show."

"No can do, lady. We're sold out. Even the house seats are gone."

It was, she told me, one of the great delights of her life.

As for me, I tried not to think about it too much. As great as all my successes had been, Broadway was really the big time. I had grave doubts about whether I belonged there.

Less than a dozen years earlier, I'd delivered tickets for the same theater at which I was now to appear. I'd stood in awe of the theater, the great performers, the great producers.

Fortunately, I had some distractions to keep me from worrying too much about such things. First of all, I had to finish my European tour. Second, I had to make sure my artists were ready for their trip.

Surprisingly, perhaps, several of the most outstanding members of my company weren't very enthusiastic about coming to the United States. The money wasn't going to be that much better than they were used to in Europe, and many of them had personal matters that needed attending to.

We had a few weeks' break before we were set to leave for America and, during that period, some of my performers began to disappear—even though I had ironclad contracts with them.

One of them went gallivanting off to Paris, another to Brussels, a third to London, another to Madrid, etc. If I didn't put a stop to this—and somehow retrieve them—I was going to be very lonely when the curtain went up at the Shubert.

I reread my performers' contracts, looking for some legal stricture that might be used to draw them back. And I found it. According to these contracts, each performer had to turn his passport over to me three weeks before departure time, so I could handle work permits and visas.

If I could get hold of those passports, I thought, I could regain control over my artists. But how could I do that? There was only one way: I'd have to go passport prospecting.

Leaving Nila, Luis, Lola, and Joaquin back in Madrid, I went off on a mission of my own—to Brussels, to Amsterdam, to Zurich, to London. In each place, I located my missing performer, then absconded with his passport.

Sometimes I had to bribe a hotel clerk to let me into a room. Sometimes I had to act the sneak thief. Sometimes I was in cahoots with a concerned relative.

It might be said that I was skirting the edges of the law, at the very least. But I didn't see it that way. I had a valid contract with each of these performers. I had every right to have possession of their passports. I wasn't going to let happen to me what happened in Paris two years before.

Once I had the passports in my hands, I phoned my performers.

"Listen, I have your passport . . .

"You what? What do you mean, I have it right here, in my . . ."

"Don't bother to look in your bag. It's in my hand right now."

"Why you bastard, you son-of-a-bitch, you thief. I'll call my embassy and I'll have you arrested, you . . ."

"Don't bother to call your embassy," I said, "your contract with me says you have to give me your passport so I can make travel arrangments. You know that."

Each time, I was met with threats and violence. My performers had found new interests, they'd met new people, they'd found new lovers. But I eventually won them over—every last one of them.

I catered to them with all the eloquence I could command. I told one that he was an undiscovered Tyrone Power, another that she could be as sensational as Ava Gardner, a third that she'd be another Rita Hayworth.

I told them about the money that was to be made in America, about movies and television, about all the wonderful opportunities.

I sent flowers, I gave wine, I passed out dinner invitations by the dozen. I was totally without shame.

After all, I was taking my company—literally—to the New World. It was as much for their benefit as mine if I persuaded those with cold feet—or other interests—that their main chance lay with me. It did. Time would prove that.

It was no simple matter, but I managed to get the whole company together again and keep them together long enough to get them on the plane to New York. Once in the United States, I felt I'd have no serious problems with them.

We arrived in New York late in September 1951, to a warm welcome by Nila's parents and mine. It was wonderful to be home—but also frightening. It was as though all the rest had only been practice.

Almost immediately after arriving, I went to meet with Lee Shubert, the same legendary Lee Shubert I'd so much admired as a young man. Shubert had bad news for me. There was, it seemed, some difficulty with the American Guild of Musical Artists—the performers' union.

According to union rules, all of my artists had to join—at an initiation fee of one hundred dollars each. I had to pay it. Then there was the monthly fee. I had to pay it. Then there was the two weeks' salary in advance. I had to pay it.

More than that, there was trouble with the Internal Revenue Service. Withholding tax had to be taken from each performer's salary every payday. But I'd agreed to pay my performers a net amount. That meant I had to pay the withholding myself—above and beyond the agreed salary.

In my naïveté, I knew nothing about union regulations. I knew nothing about the withholding tax. Remember, I'd left the United States in 1945, when taxes were a simpler matter. When I found out about these things, it was rough going.

Rajah Margo, had she been well, might have known, might have been able to advise me to have my contract with Shubert cover such things. But she was desperately ill in Copenhagen, unable to advise.

Shubert advanced me twelve thousand dollars—the first two weeks' fees. This allowed me to cover the union bond and pay the performers' withholding taxes. But it put me in the hole, perhaps permanently. I had nothing.

Fortunately, I did have Mama and her macaroni and her spaghetti, and also Nila's parents, who lent their support. Without them all, I don't know how Nila and I would have kept body and soul together.

"Don't worry, José," Shubert told me. "You're going to have a great success. We've made sure about that. In a few weeks, your money worries will be over, watch and see."

I wasn't so confident. In fact, I was terrified. True, I'd played to millions of people since last I performed in New York. But these were European audiences. I understood Europe. I had an affinity with Europe. America seemed impregnable.

We had two days to set up and prepare—opening night was October 1. As I came and went, I saw my name up there in lights. I saw my picture (and pictures of the other performers in my company) on lobby cards and displays. And I heard people talking about me.

"Jesus," they'd say, "this guy must be another Nijinsky."

"He'd better be. He's going to be in New York a full month."

I wasn't Nijinsky. I could only do five or six great "breaks." I could only do a couple of turns on my knee. I could tap only with my heels. I could only throw myself across the stage a few times. I could only take a stance of great authority.

That was it, and it wasn't enough. Not for American audiences. They wouldn't be impressed. They wouldn't fall for it. They could rise up and destroy me.

To succeed in America, you had to be Ina Claire, you had to be Alec Guinness, you had to be Laurence Olivier or Vivien Leigh, you had to be a Noël Coward or a Billy Rose or a Lee Shubert.

Who was I, an immigrant from Montorio, a kid from Brooklyn who never finished high school, a ticket runner? What right had I to be on Broadway?

NINETEEN

The preparations for our opening went well enough. Shubert and I talked at length about technical matters such as curtains and lighting, and about which numbers might be cut and which lengthened and which artists should be featured and which de-emphasized.

Yet I still worried about every detail. I looked at the decors and I couldn't decide whether they were perfect—or completely wrong. I watched the final run-throughs and couldn't be sure if the show flowed smoothly or was jarringly disjointed. Small things went wrong, and I saw them as catastrophes.

Luckily, I did not have too much time to ruminate. Before I knew it, opening night was upon us. I was backstage, peering out at the audience through a crack in the curtains.

The eighteen-hundred-seat theater was filling rapidly. Mama and Poppa were there, along with Nila's parents, along with a number of family friends, and friends and relatives of some of the other performers in the show.

Most of the faces I saw, of course, I did not know. And among them were New York's newspaper reviewers, there to cast a critical eye at what I had created. Would they praise me or would they damn me? I hadn't the slightest idea.

Then the orchestra began to play, the curtain opened, and we were on. As my company and I began to dance, I could feel the doubts and fears disappearing. I knew what I was doing, I knew I could dance, I knew I'd mastered the pacing of a show. I knew I could entertain.

And when our first number came to an end, it was instantly clear that the audience knew, too. We were met by a crash of applause that set the chandeliers tinkling, and there were several shouts of "Bravo!"

So it went—my company and I performing our hearts out, the audience roaring out its approval. As the show wore on, I began to realize that a rare rapport, almost an identity of purpose, was being established between artists and audience.

We danced to excite and inflame, to show our viewers how beautiful we were, to display the emotions that drove us. The audience responded in kind, understanding our intent completely. It not only approved of our efforts, it also loved us passionately.

We stayed up that night waiting for the reviews, as so many performers do. But my fears had vanished. I knew it would be the way it had been in Seville, in Paris, in Copenhagen. And I wasn't disappointed.

"At the opening of a play, the audience is usually quite sedate," wrote Robert Coleman in the *Daily Mirror*. "But not so Latin dance fans. Several recognized and approached us, exclaiming with excitement, 'It's terrific,' 'It's marvelous,' 'It's great!'

"And they were right. Greco has style and polish. His every movement on stage drew salvos of applause."

Then there was Walter Terry, in the *Herald Tribune*:

"Greco has managed to fuse the elements of a dance recital with those of a popular review, and he has done this without lowering the high standards of Spanish dance itself.

"He is a shrewd director, a gifted choreographer, a highly sensitive artist, an engaging performer and he has fearlessly surrounded himself with artists worthy of him and the dance form he cherishes.

"The star—and he is just that—brings to his dancing a handsome presence, a fine sense of body line good for the projection of lyrical measures as well as for reflecting the graceful pride of the Spaniard in motion. Intensity . . . is ever felt."

And Frances Herridge, of the New York *Post*, wrote this:

"A month of one program is an unprecedented run for the Spanish dance, but if any company can sustain it, this one should. The program has something of everything Spanish—classic, folk and flamenco. There's plenty of passion, even a comic sketch.

"There's not a dull moment in the evening. It's no wonder that Europe loved them. The males are entirely masculine, the women are full-blooded and irresistible.

"Greco himself is better than he was with Argentinita over six years ago. His movements have the snap of a whip, particularly his knee and foot work. His style is a blend of elegance and strength."

Wrote Robert Baker, another New York reviewer:

"The troupe is most entertaining—sometimes genial, sometimes electric. Virtually all the dancing, whatever its type, I found completely engrossing.

"There's no denying Mr. Greco has remarkable gifts. As a younger dancer with the late, lamented Argentinita, he was refreshingly fleet and precise. Today, a mature artist, and, what's more, a compelling choreographer, Mr. Greco is, by any standards, the one great star of the show.

"He has magnetism almost in excess. He has wonderful variety in his dancing, in his expressions—from the tortured and strained to the utterly ecstatic.

"It would be hard to forget, for instance, Mr. Greco's astonishing performance in the Millers' Dance, which was pictorially beautiful, all force and intensity. . . ."

Naturally, I was overjoyed with what the reviewers said about me. Ever since I first realized what Broadway was, back in the mid-1930s, I'd longed to be part of it. Now, at the age of thirty-two, I was.

Yet I felt a strange depression that day, perhaps the natural result of the intense anxieties I'd just experienced. I'd keyed myself up for the biggest battle of my life—and I'd won. But I was still keyed up and I didn't know what to do with my energy now. This ultimate glory had left me with a certain sense of loneliness.

Fortunately, there were distractions. The morning after we opened, I got a telegram from an old friend—Jack Nonnenbacher, the agent who'd advised me, years ago, to become a truck driver. "Will be in front row center with June Lockhart October 3," he wired, from St. Louis.

Sure enough, on the appointed night, he and June Lockhart, the movie star, were there, out in front. The next day, we all went to lunch together at Sardi's.

"I always knew you'd make it, José," Nonnenbacher said.

"You always knew it? Don't you remember telling me Spanish dancers were a dime a dozen, that I should drive a truck?"

Nonnenbacher looked at me wryly, picked up his coffee cup, and somehow got the saucer caught between two fingers. We watched nervously, sure he was going to make a mess. Then he broke into a big grin—it had all been an act.

"We all make mistakes, don't we?"

I think that Jack, in bringing June, may have been matchmaking, not realizing I was married. I did find her a beautiful, even sublime woman. Though there was never a question of romance between us, we established a wonderful relationship.

But Jack's company was even more important to me. He was unfailingly charming and witty. He had a rare ability to make people laugh, whatever the circumstances. More than that, his knowledge of the world and his intellect were truly stupendous.

That lunch did more than simply renew an old acquaintanceship. It began a profound friendship, based on mutual respect and admiration. From that moment on, Jack Nonnenbacher was one of the pillars of my life. In a very real sense, he became part of my family.

Often he'd invite me and some of the members of my company out after our performance. We'd go to such places as Billy Reed's Little Club. There we met Jack's great friend Dan Dailey, and the three of us—Dan, Billy Reed, and I, would do a real show—three hoofers on the stage. Of course, no one knew I didn't know the classic time steps so important to tap dancing. But I gave a Spanish flair to the little show and the audience was delighted with our improvisations.

During this period, I also renewed my acquaintance with Fredric March and his wife, Florence Eldridge. Through them and George Macy, I met Katharine Cornell and her director-producer husband, Guthrie McClintock, Jane Powell, Ina Claire, Raymond Massey, and many others—all of whom had been legends to me.

Now I found myself chatting with these people, people whom I'd put on pedestals years ago. Even as I talked with them, I told myself it was impossible. But it was very possible and very real. This was the world I had entered.

We were scarcely two weeks into our run at the Shubert when Lee Shubert realized we should be extended for another month. But we could not stay where we were. Cole Porter's new musical, *Can-Can*, was set to open there on November 1.

So Shubert moved us to the even larger theater, the Century, on Fifty-ninth Street and Seventh Avenue—a spot now occupied by a beautiful apartment house. And there, too, we played to standing-room only.

During this period, my parents saw the show almost every night, coming down from the Bronx by subway or taxi. Mama, always the extrovert, told anyone who'd listen that I was her son. She overflowed with pride.

After the theater, when we went out to eat, at Sardi's or Vesuvio or some other famous restaurant, usually accompanied by eminent people, she'd join us and boast cockily about my success.

Naturally, Mama and I recalled those horrendous arguments we'd had in Brooklyn, in which she'd said I'd wind up a bum and I'd told her she'd have cause to change her mind someday, someday.

Now I admitted that she'd been right—that if she hadn't criticized and provoked me, I never would have been the star that I had become. This was true. She'd instilled in me a pride, a need to accomplish.

After these Broadway dinners, I'd corner Mama and say, "Now, listen, Mama, here's twenty dollars. I want you and Poppa to take a taxi back home, because it's late. I don't want you taking the subway."

And she'd say, "That's very nice of you, Costanzo, thank you very much."

I didn't know it until later, but Jack Nonnenbacher had the identical conversation with Mama every night. So did Joaquin. So did Nila. And so did Norina, when she was there.

By the time she and Poppa were ready to go, Mama had usually collected a hundred dollars. And this was every night, for nearly two months. Did she take a taxi then? Of course not. She took the subway. She was convinced it was the safest way to travel.

Bit by bit, all of this money came back to those who'd given it to her, in the form of a beautiful coat for Nila or Norina, a beautiful jacket for Joaquin or Jack, a gift for me. Mama would have done anything for her children, or those who were devoted to her children. I'll never forget her for this.

During my New York run, a number of famous people came backstage to see me. Among the first was Ed Sullivan.

"I remember when you were with Argentinita, José. I believe I mentioned you in my column once. It's nice to see you doing so well."

"Thank you very much, Mr. Sullivan."

"Now, I want you to appear on my television show. . . ."

Through the auspices of the William Morris Agency (with whom I'd worked before, when Nila and I toured New England), it was arranged. We performed two numbers, for a fee of three thousand dollars—not too bad in those days. It was the first of many appearances for me on the Sullivan show.

While I was performing at the Century Theater, two movie

producers came to see me. The first was Louis B. Mayer, accompanied by Gene Kelly. At the time, they were preparing the movie *Invitation to the Dance,* and they wanted me to appear in it.

Unfortunately, I was unable to accept their offer, because of my tour commitments. This happened many times in my life, but there was nothing I could do about it. I had to get bookings far in advance —to assure my security and hold my company together—and once I had these bookings, they could not be canceled.

The next movie producer to see me was Samuel Goldwyn. A newspaperman was present at the time, and he recorded our conversation:

Goldwyn (to a Greco assistant): "Please tell Señor Greco that I enjoyed his performance very much."
Greco: "Thank you very much, Mr. Goldwyn."
Goldwyn: "What? You speak English?"
Greco: "Yes, I do. I should—I was raised in Brooklyn."
Goldwyn: "Will you listen to that? The guy speaks better English than I do."

Goldwyn wanted me to choreograph a movie he was about to make—*Hans Christian Andersen.* If I accepted the job, he would extend Andersen's visit to Spain and insert several dances. Much as I wanted to do it, the date of this filming, too, conflicted with my tour.

Before we left New York, I was notified that Carol Channing and I had been selected as "New Broadway Personalities of the Year" by an important theater group. We were honored at a party filled with Broadway personalities. How could I doubt now that I truly belonged?

Just before we closed, Nila began having trouble with her health again. This time the problem seemed relatively simple—ingrown nails on her two big toes.

She had relatively minor surgery to relieve the pain, but this forced her to miss our last few performances in New York. Even as we headed toward our next stop—Boston—her pain continued.

The Boston papers did their best to prepare that center of culture for our arrival. The Boston *Advertiser,* for instance, discussed the history of Spanish dance in a November 25 article.

"The sultry Austrian dancer, Fanny Essler, a student of Delores Soral, of the Royal Theater of Madrid, first introduced the Spanish dance to Europe and North America in 1834. She toured the world for 15 years, demonstrating her art.

"(One critic) wrote of her, 'She darts forward, the castanets begin their sonorous clatter. With her hands, she seems to shake clusters of rhythm. How she twists! How she bends! What fire, what voluptuousness of motion!'

"Many years later, she was followed in New York by José Otero, considered by many the father of today's Spanish choreography. Then came La Meri [Nila's teacher], the ethnic dancer from Louisville, Kentucky. She was followed by the fabulous Escudero, the lovely Argentina, the magnificent Argentinita—and now, José Greco."

We opened in Boston on December 1, for a two-week stay. Our reception was a mirror image of what had happened to us in New York. Both audiences and critics hailed us, singling me out for special praise.

Said Peggy Doyle, writing in the Boston *Evening American*, "Greco, of course, is the star. Possibly his finest performance and the show's finest offering is El Cortijo, in which he and three assisting men dancers convey the rhythm and sound of horsement, in an exultant, inspiring number. As always, he is the Spaniard at his graceful, prideful best. He has elegance, vitality and handsomeness."

Elliott Norton, of the Boston *Post*, seconded the motion: "Straight and slim, Greco has the catlike grace and the floating likeness of a swan on water. In movement or pose, the line of his body has a classic quality, true and graceful, without strain or stress."

And the Boston *Globe* had similar praise: "Greco is tall, dark and alive. He has a powerful technique and a polished style. It is not quite exact to say that he excels in one dance or another, for all his work has individuality and makes a spectacular impression."

From Boston we went on to Philadelphia, where we were once more greeted with full houses and critical acclaim. Said the *Evening Bulletin*, "Greco has a personality of great magnetism. He is tall, slim as a sapling and moves with grace and authority. He has all the sinewy grace of a toreador."

After two great weeks in Philadelphia, we went on to Pittsburgh, to the Nixon Theater. "Spanish dancers offer fine show," the headlines read. "Almost flawless exhibition."

After Pittsburgh came Washington, D.C., as we headed into 1952.

There, the *Times-Herald* went out of its way to prepare audiences for what they were about to see, with a little history lesson.

"Spanish dancing is older than any other form of European dance art," the paper said. "It goes back to 500 B.C. At that time, lady dancers from Cadiz were already wandering across foreign borders to delight neighboring countries.

"Spanish dancing can be traced back to India and Persia. It contains strong traces of the choreography and music of the Arabic, Byzantine and Hebrew.

"The dance music of Spain is totally distinct from all other Western nations. It is divided into four separate styles: regional, flamenco, classic and renaissance. The regional dances contain hundreds of communal dances, each with its own tuneful music and elaborate bright costumes."

After we opened, this critic had a great deal to say about our performance. "José Greco has included as many of the various forms and styles of Spanish dancing as he is able to crowd into a single evening. The brilliant dancer/choreographer is a top artist and you'd have to look far to find his equal.

"He has assembled a supporting company which, while they cannot match his regal authority, prove to be charming, ingratiating performers. The fluid grace, the slower, statelier choreography, the exuberance of the company, the sense of comedy and the many individual performances add up to a uniquely enthralling experience."

We then went on to Detroit, where we played at the Masonic Temple—the same place at which I'd washed dishes while waiting to get a job at the Ford plant.

It's hard to express how much of a thrill this was for me. There, on the same walls on which I'd seen plastered the posters of Menuhin, Segovia, and Rubinstein, I now saw my own face.

From an artistic and commercial point of view, Detroit was a repeat of what had happened elsewhere since I'd arrived in the United States. The reviews were fabulous, the audiences incredibly responsive, the theater filled.

We arrived in Chicago at the end of January, and opened very successfully. But at least one person in town wasn't pleased to see us—Claudia Cassidy, critic for the *Tribune*.

The day before we'd opened, she wrote, "Okay, folks, the Spanish castanets are coming into town. Don't forget to stay away, because this fellow Greco can never match the great Escudero."

And after we opened, she wrote, "Just as I predicted, Greco is the worst Spanish dancer on the stage today. Go at your own risk."

What caused this hostility, I do not know. I'd never met the woman. Perhaps it had something to do with a long-standing affection for Escudero. Or maybe she felt no Italian kid from Brooklyn could ever be a Spanish dancer, regardless of what they thought in Seville.

Fortunately, she was alone in her view. Ann Barzell, writing in the Chicago *Herald-American*, expressed the majority opinion when she said,

"José Greco . . . is a dancer whose movements and style are so attractive that if he merely walked around the stage, that would be satisfying. Not that he does that. His whip-sharp turns, the way he slides across the stage on one knee, his staccato heel beats and his overall polish are a pleasure to behold."

On this occasion, anyhow, the residents of Chicago ignored the powerful *Tribune*. They came to the theater in great, huge mobs. Our engagement was extended once, then again.

But Chicago was the last stop on our tour.

With the coming of March, my six-month contract with Shubert would be over. He'd implied that it would be renewed, that there was no problem. Now, I waited.

While we were playing in Chicago, a Shubert representative came to see me, all smiles.

"Well, Mr. Greco, I have a new contract for you to sign."

"Fine. I was expecting it."

He handed me the document. "You'll notice that it is for the 1953–54 season."

"What?"

"That's right. It begins the October after next."

"The October after next? Why, that's a year and a half away. What am I supposed to do, what is my company supposed to do until then?"

"I imagine Mr. Shubert thought you might want to return to Europe."

"Europe? That would cost me a fortune. Besides, I haven't any bookings there. I thought I would continue with the Shubert theaters here."

"Well, you will. But not this year. Our analysts have studied the situation and they've decided it would be better to give it a rest for one full season."

"Maybe that's fine for Mr. Shubert, but that isn't so good for me."

"Yes," the representative said. "I see your problem. Well, perhaps you could make a movie."

I considered this. According to our agreement, Shubert got 50 per cent of any movie fee I was paid while I was under contract to him. For the first time, I began to think about what that meant.

It meant that if I were paid, say, fifty thousand dollars, I'd get only twenty-five thousand dollars—and out of this, I'd have to pay my taxes, my expenses, my agent's fees, etc. What would I have left? I'd end up with nothing.

This is what happened to another Shubert star, Carmen Miranda. She made dozens of films and was paid handsomely—but died penniless. Those visits from Mayer and Goldwyn hadn't been accidental. The Shuberts had arranged for them. Only circumstances saved me.

"Well, all right," I told the Shubert representative. "I'll sign the contract. I'll just arrange for my own bookings during the interim."

"Arrange for your own? Do you mean here, in the United States?"

"Of course. I can't afford to take the company back to Europe."

"That would violate the contract, Mr. Greco. Only Mr. Shubert can present you in the United States."

"So, according to this contract, I cannot work."

"You could put it that way, I suppose. At least that's the case in the United States."

"And if I ignore the contract?"

"That would be very grave, Mr. Greco. If you break the contract, you'll be billed for your original transportation expenses, for publicity expenses, for decors and settings. . . ."

"But I thought Shubert paid for those things."

"Only for someone under contract."

It was an impossible choice. Whatever I did, I went broke. But if I went off on my own, at least I had a chance. It was a hell of a way to start out, deeply in debt to Shubert, without any bookings. But it was the only way.

I had a name now. José Greco meant something in the United States. Did it mean enough? I would soon find out.

TWENTY

Soon after the Shubert representative left, I picked up the phone and called my contact at the William Morris Agency, a man named Klaus Kolmar.

I told him what had happened with Shubert. "Klaus, what I need is bookings. Can you do anything for me?"

"I do know of one thing," he said. "Olson and Johnson—you know, that crazy comedy team—are bringing their *Hellzapoppin'* show into the Palace next month. They need another act on the bill. Would you be interested?"

"At this point, Klaus, I'd be interested in anything."

"Fine. I'll take care of the details."

Now, at least, there was something in the future. What worried me, though, was the fear that I'd get myself into another situation like the one with Shubert. I needed competent advice.

When I'd been approached by Goldwyn and Mayer, I'd engaged Arnold Weisberger and Aaron Frosch, New York's top show business lawyers. They represented Elizabeth Taylor, Rex Harrison, Marilyn Monroe, and a hundred other top people.

Now, however, I needed something beyond legal advice. I called my friend Jack Nonnenbacher, thinking he might have some ideas. From his years of experience with Baron Singer's Midgets and Paul Haakon, among others, he knew show business inside out.

"What you need, José, is a personal manager, to handle your affairs, to take care of money matters, to arrange transportation and everything else."

"Yes, but where would I find such a man?"

"You happen to be talking to such a man."

He was right—he was the perfect one. "Are you willing?"

"Willing and eager."

"Well, I guess I've gotten myself a personal manager," I said. Already, I felt better.

The next month, the José Greco dance company opened at the Palace Theater, in New York, in tandem with Olson and Johnson. It was not a felicitous pairing. In fact, it was a disaster.

Of course, I should have learned how audiences respond to a pairing of unlike things when Norina sang opera and I danced in Madrid. Half the program is ignored by at least half the audience. But it took this second, painful lesson to get the message through to me.

By this time, Jack had found me another booking agent, Charlie Green, who was well known in the concert field. Green got us some scattered bookings across the United States and we struggled away, moving steadily toward the West Coast.

Unfortunately, without the Shubert organization behind us, we didn't have the proper promotion or advertising. We didn't have the cash to mount any sort of publicity campaign.

In each city we played that spring, we lost money rather than making it. Philadelphia, Pittsburgh, Detroit, Chicago, St. Louis, Denver, Kansas City, Salt Lake City, Seattle—none was outstanding; several were catastrophic.

Jack and I spent long hours talking about my troubles. By this time, we were right on the edge of bankruptcy. The United States, which had once seemed so promising, was turning out to be a kind of Death Valley so far as we were concerned.

Ahead of us lay San Francisco's Curran Theater, and Los Angeles, San Diego, and several other cities in the Southwest. But we had an old, familiar problem—not enough cash in the till to make the trip.

We found an old, familiar solution: Norina. She came up with three thousand. June Lockhart matched my sister's contribution. June's was an outright loan. Norina, with her money, bought 25 per cent of the José Greco Company, Inc. (Both later got back every penny, and Norina's investment paid off very handsomely.)

Well, we put all of our eggs in one basket. We spent all we had getting to San Francisco and publicizing our forthcoming appearance there. It was do or die for the José Greco company. If we failed in San Francisco, we'd have to go back to Europe and continue however we could.

But San Francisco was a repeat of our New York experience. We opened to a full house, elicited marvelous audience response and sensational reviews. Our original two weeks were extended to four, during which time we grossed about $150,000—smashing every known record for the theater.

After that month, I went on my old, familiar errands—paying off debts. We were alive again. Without any help from the Shubert organization, we'd made a marvelous success in America.

With money enough to pay for promotion, we were able to repeat our San Francisco success in Los Angeles, in San Diego, and throughout the southwestern United States. As spring came to an end, the José Greco company was an attraction to be reckoned with.

In Los Angeles, a movie agent found me and asked if he could represent me in Hollywood. I agreed. Shortly afterward, I found myself doing a screen test. It was not an encouraging experience.

In a screen test, all the subject does—for the most part—is sit and talk about himself, while the cameras shoot him from every possible angle. I remember the conversation I had during my screen test:

"Can you tap dance, Mr. Greco?"

"No."

"How about singing. Can you sing?"

"No, I'm not a singer."

"Well, let's go on to acting. Have you ever done any acting?"

"No, not really. I don't hoof, I don't sing, I don't act—I'm a flamenco dancer, and that's it."

Then they had me do a solo, then a dance with Nila.

Frankly, I expected nothing whatever to come of this. I knew my test would be passed around to all the Hollywood studios—that's the way it's done. And I thought they'd give it a big yawn and forget about me.

But, to my surprise, my agent soon had good news for me.

"We've had an offer from MGM," he told me. The famous director, Jack Cummings, saw the screen test. "They're making a film called *Sombrero*, and they want you to be in it."

"What role am I supposed to play?"

"You'll be a bullfighter and a dancer."

I wasn't overwhelmed.

152

"Listen, José, you'll be starring along with Cyd Charisse and Ricardo Montalban."

My agent finally convinced me to accept. The picture was to be shot in Mexico, in the late summer of 1952—the perfect time, since it was before our fall tour started.

Among other things, it gave me a chance to spend some time in Europe. I had to see the Maestro. He'd left the company for a few months, to take on a high-paying accompanist's job. Now I wanted to sign him to a contract for the coming season.

Nila and I went back to Madrid and I went on to Paris, to see the Maestro. When I came back to Madrid, I heard some disturbing rumors about Nila's brother, Luis Olivares, and Lola de Ronda.

A few months earlier, Carola Goya had left our company, leaving Luis and Lola to establish whatever relationship came naturally. And, naturally, that relationship was a romance. Nila and I were pleased, since Luis and Lola were a far better match than Luis and Carola had been. But we had no idea just how hot this new romance had become.

We found out in Spain. Luis and Lola had taken advantage of their time off to go to Copenhagen. Then, Luis had headed back for the States, and Lola had returned to Spain. All of this seemed innocent enough, but something about it bothered me.

I felt a certain responsibility to Lola—and to her family. After all, I'd hired her away from Pilar Lopez. I'd promised her mother that I'd keep an eye on her and make sure she was taken care of, as if she were a member of my family. It was a promise I'd meant, a promise I thought I'd kept.

Hearing that Lola was back in Madrid, I went to her family's apartment, to say hello to her and to find out what was going on between her and Luis. I knocked on the door, and Lola's mother opened it.

As soon as she realized who was standing there, she reared back and gave me such a sock that I was flung back against the hallway wall. "You bastard! You son-of-a-bitch! You liar! You promised me you'd take care of Lola, and now look what's happened!"

I was dazed. I shook my head to clear out the cobwebs. "What do you mean? What's happened to Lola? Where is she? Is she all right?"

"Wouldn't you like to know where she is, you son-of-a-bitch! Wouldn't you like to get her in trouble again!"

"Get her in trouble? What are you talking about?"

"Don't you pretend, you bastard! You know what's happened. Your fucking brother-in-law, Luis, promised my daughter he'd marry her, then he got her pregnant. Then he said he wasn't going to marry her, and he took her to Copenhagen to get rid of the baby. Don't tell me you don't know!"

"So help me God, I didn't. Listen, is she all right? Where is she?"

"She's recuperating in a little town on the Mediterranean and she's okay—no thanks to you."

"I wish I could tell you how sorry I am that this has happened. Please forgive me. Give me a chance to make everything right."

"What? I should forgive you? Everybody knows about you, José Greco. Your performers abandon you at the slightest excuse. Your company is filled with whores and pimps."

"That's not so. . . ."

"Don't you lie to me, you whoremaster! We've heard all the stories. Do you think we all live in locked rooms?"

"What stories?"

Lola's mother then proceeded to tell me a dozen tales of degradation, thievery, and immorality, each worse than the last. Furthermore, they were all true—but not of my company.

What she'd heard—and imputed to the José Greco dance company—was a collection of horrible stories that had happened to various lesser outfits. There were dozens of Spanish dance companies touring the world by this time. Because mine was the most famous and my name was the best known, gossipers eager to inflate the value of their inside information always said these things had happened to my company.

Somehow, apologizing profusely and explaining as best I could, I talked my way inside the door. Here, I knew, was the story that would make all the rest believable—if it got out. I had to prevent that. Also, there was the question of Luis and Lola. They were vital to my company at this time. I couldn't afford to part with either of them. I had to make peace with Lola's mother.

I pleaded, I begged, I cajoled. I assured Lola's mother that I would make sure nothing further happened to blacken the reputation of her innocent lamb. I swore that I would talk to Luis and make him behave. She let me in, still suspicious.

"Let me prove it to you," she said.

"No, no, I believe you."

She walked into the bedroom and came out with an enormous packet of letters—there must have been fifty of them. There were letters between Lola and her mother and between Luis and Lola. It was a complete collection of the last six months' correspondence, in both directions.

"Read. See your brother-in-law's perfidy for yourself."

Believe it or not, we spent the better part of three days reading these letters, arguing over them, analyzing them in excruciating detail. She wanted me to know the truth, the exact truth, even though I protested that I already did.

Well, I was wrong. So was Lola's mother. I found a paragraph in one of Lola's letters to Luis that revealed she wasn't the innocent child I'd thought.

"Just because I lost my virginity when I was a youngster," she told Luis, "that doesn't mean I love you any less."

I called this to the attention of Lola's mother. "See," I said, treading gingerly, "your daughter wasn't exactly an innocent."

"Of course not," her mother said. "You knew that. What does that have to do with anything?"

"I knew that? What makes you think I knew that? I didn't know. I had no idea."

"What utter nonsense! Don't you start lying to me again."

"It's a complete surprise to me, I promise you."

Now I began to see what might have been the cause of the trouble between Luis and Lola. She'd told him she was a virgin. When it turned out she wasn't, he felt betrayed. I said as much to her mother who, while she wasn't ready to admit this, wasn't able to deny it, either. It was my turn to take the offensive.

"You know," I said, "there's nothing wrong with Lola now. She's doing well with my company, she's earning a good living, she's well accepted on stage."

"So you say. But she has been violated."

"Well, that can happen to anybody. But there's no need for scandal or shame. No one else need ever know about this, you know. Everything can be as before."

"Do you expect me to entrust my daughter to you again?" she said bitterly. "After what you let happen?"

155

"Let's get that straight. You're the one who let it happen. You brought her up. It's not my fault if your daughter had hot pants."

This time, Lola's mother had nothing to say.

"Now I'm going to talk to Lola," I said, "and I'm going to do my best to convince her to come back to my company, because I need her and because that's where she belongs."

"I don't know."

"Well, if she doesn't come back to me, what do you think will happen to her?"

Lola's mother shrugged. She knew I was right.

"I don't expect you to give me your blessing. You did that once, and I couldn't live up to it. Just give me your approval. Now that I know the true state of affairs, I'll do my best to protect Lola. I'll talk to her, and I'll talk to Luis."

She nodded.

"And I'll accept your slap and your emotional outburst as something very Latin, something meant for someone else."

"Okay, José," she said. "But please, do what you can to protect her. See if you can get Luis to respond to her love—I know she loves him."

"I'll do my best—but only time can tell."

Now I sought out Lola, to convince her to return. It wasn't easy. She said that if she couldn't get Luis Olivares to marry her, she wasn't going to go back to America.

I managed to persuade her that coming back was the best thing she could do, both personally and professionally. "As for Luis, you should forget him. Forget what happened to you—it could happen to anyone."

"Maybe you're right, Chief," she said. (Everyone in the company called me that.)

Then I looked up Luis. "Listen, Luis, you're causing me tremendous problems because of what's going on between you and Lola. If you love each other, fine. Otherwise, don't screw around—find yourself someone else. Do you understand?"

"Well, I'm a human being, you know. I operate on my emotions most of the time."

"I understand. Otherwise I wouldn't need to talk to you. I'm just asking you to control yourself—for your own good."

"Okay, José. Fine. I'll do as you say."

It had been a very difficult situation, fraught with both personal